THE
GIFT
OF THE
DEVIL

AND EMBRACING
HIS INDISPENSABLE ROLE

A JOURNAL BY:

EMILY AYARS SMITH

The Gift of the Devil

To request permissions, contact the publisher at
freedomhousepublishingco@gmail.com or
emilyayars@gmail.com.
Paperback ISBN: 978-1-952566-17-2
Ebook ISBN: 978-1-952566-23-3
Printed in the USA.
Freedom House Publishing Co
Middleton, ID 83644
www.freedomhousepublishingco.com

FREEDOM HOUSE
PUBLISHING CO

Introduction

The human body is a fascinating thing. Having studied the eye for a brief time in college anatomy, I learned something that has always stuck with me. When looking at an object, we are actually looking at the light that is reflected from that object. The light comes through the front of the eye called the cornea. The pupil, which is surrounded by the colored part of the eye (iris), adjusts the amount of light that comes into the eye. Since the front part of the eye is curved like a spoon, it bends the light. This creates an upside-down image on the back of the eye called the retina. When the image is relayed to the brain via the retina, the brain will turn the image the "right" way up.[1] If this brain function was not working as it should the world would seem so alien. Mountains would look as though they were falling out of the sky and people would appear to be walking on the ceiling. The fact alone that the brain knows to turn the image so it all makes sense to us is astonishing.

The physical phenomenon of light entering through the eye and the brain's ability to flip the image around mirrors the behavior of a very real spiritual phenomenon; that is a person's ability to give meaning to what is seen. Specifically, it is the act of innately labeling something as "good" or "bad," being

---

[1] "The Eyes: Protecting Sight." *Sightsavers*, 12 Oct. 2020, www.sightsavers.org/protecting-sight/the-eyes/.

able to flip, or change, the meaning of what is originally seen to mean something else.

When thoughts and beliefs are attached to what is seen, emotions follow - like peace, fear, excitement, or anger. It is a function we have inherited from our primal ancestors. It is the deep subconscious, or the reptilian brain, in charge of ensuring our survival. Whether it is an actual threat or an imaginary one, the reptilian brain triggers reactions in the body needed to protect itself or run away [2]. It's all about survival. It is the reason a person walking on a trail may jump in fear after confusing a rope for a snake.

In my limited learning about how the human brain works, and learning how humans have used stories (like Adam and Eve in the Garden of Eden) to animate this process of determining good vs. bad, I have made a powerful shift in mindset that has helped me manipulate this process for my ultimate benefit.

In this book, I will first discuss the natural functions of the human brain and how God uses those brain systems to communicate with us. Communing with God comes by way of two contrasting characters: the Devil and Jesus Christ. In this I will convey that not only does working the Atonement save, but that only through the Devil can we actually find the answers we seek. That is why the Devil's purpose is a gift. I will also include additional spiritual concepts and a powerful way to view them. Next, I will share my own personal experiences of how I used the gift of the Devil and Atonement to become free from depression, anxiety, and the chains of childhood beliefs that had been my "Rules to Live By" and

---

[2] Komninos, Andreas. "Our Three Brains - The Reptilian Brain." *The Interaction Design Foundation*, Mar. 2020, www.interaction-design.org/literature/article/our-three-brains-the-reptilian-brain.

unknowingly controlled all outcomes of my experiences - without my knowledge. Last, I will speak on the importance of taking on this new outlook and how to move forward as creators - living your best life!

I feel it's important to say here that if there is significant trauma in your life due to abuse or other forms of neglect, a professional psychologist, therapist, or counselor should aid you in the healing process. There are some hardships that require guidance from someone with specialized tools and experience in order to overcome them. I have been truly blessed by seeking help as I've used this process to heal from my own personal hardships and traumas. You do not have to go it alone.

Table of Contents

CHAPTER 1

"The Gift of The Devil"

The 3 Systems of the Brain

To understand the gift of the Devil it's extremely helpful to first study the way we as humans process information in the brain. I mentioned earlier the workings of the human eye and its unique functions. Studying the brain in the same light can help us understand the grand workings of ourselves. Realizing how the brain works will help us understand how spiritual concepts align with this process.

We as human beings are a very complex species. American physician and neuroscientist Paul D. MacLean made huge contributions in brain research from Yale Medical School and the National Institute of Mental Health. Without getting too technical, he discovered that there are 3 main brain systems that control behavior. Just as the word control suggests, these are automatic reactions. The names of these systems come layered in the brain. The first (most inner part) is what is known as the reptilian brain, the second is the limbic system, and the third is the neocortex. These systems of the brain work interdependently, meaning they all talk to each other and are activated based on whatever system is talking.

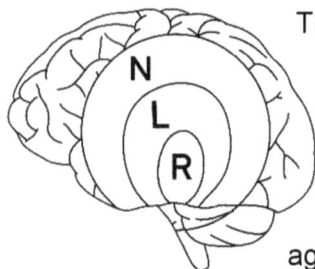

The reptilian brain controls the body's vital functions such as heart rate, breathing, body temperature, and balance. The limbic system is in charge of recording memories of behaviors that produce either agreeable or disagreeable results; thus it is in charge of all our emotions. This is also where our values and judgements are created, often unconsciously. The neocortex is the reason we have language, abstract thought, imagination and consciousness.

These systems work with each other for our survival and safety. For example, the limbic system can activate the reptilian brain. If we mistake a rope for a snake on a Saturday morning hike, our hearts will beat faster, we may begin to sweat, and hormones are released to prepare our bodies to run because we remember that snakes can bite and sometimes kill. This process works to regulate our bodies for whatever situation is at hand. In another scenario, you may be watching a movie that is emotionally upsetting. You know that the images are not real, they are pixels on a screen, but your neocortex takes an upsetting, abstract image and tells the limbic system which triggers an emotional response as though it were real. Likewise, you could be lying in bed one night and start imagining an upsetting scenario. Your partner left the house to pick up a gallon of milk from the store. You text them a message, but an hour goes by and there's no response. Then you think they must be dead! They were hit by a car or mugged in the parking lot! A distant siren blares by the house. Then you think the ambulance is for them! At this point, all systems are activated. This imaginary scenario triggers the emotional response of anxiety so your heart beats faster and you can't peacefully fall asleep until they walk through the door

- perhaps not even then. In these cases, all three systems are communicating with each other.[3]

As we get older and start to develop beliefs and judgements based on the emotional pairings assigned by the limbic system, those beliefs and judgements in our minds turn into our reality. We think of them as facts. We become fixed in the mindset of right and wrong. We become less flexible and our minds are harder to change. Habits are formed and our true natures are manipulated, shaped and changed like clay. This is great for protecting us from lions or snakes, but not so helpful when trying to overcome imagined fears or abstract threats. In all, it limits personal growth.

Why is this process so important to understand? Bottom line: if we understand how our brains work, we will understand how God uses that process to speak to us. So, in relation to the brain, where is God found?

The Space Where God Is

Thoughts have the potential to create all kinds of emotional responses that lead to all kinds of decision making. It's also important to note that because we are humans with emotions and imagination, we often take our experiences and turn them into future judgements, sometimes without even realizing it because they were founded in childhood. We do this because our emotions trigger the same regulatory process as seeing a snake would. If trauma has happened in the past, it is stored

---

[3] Sapolsky, Robert. "3 Brain Systems That Control Your Behavior: Reptilian, Limbic, Neo Cortex." *YouTube*, 25 June 2017, www.youtube.com/watch?v=hg6XUYWj-pk&feature=youtu.be.

and remembered in the body. That's why it can be so difficult to overcome learned behavior - it's automatic.

STIMULUS ⇨ (CHOICE) ⇨ OUR RESPONSE

Most importantly, knowing that the brain works in this way, one can feel more in control. Yes, these are automatic responses, but as Viktor E. Frankl (neurologist and Holocaust survivor) has taught, "Between stimulus and response there is a space. In that space is our power to choose our response. In our response lies our growth and our freedom." In this space is where we can question our thoughts. Yes, we may experience fear and anxiety, but in this space is where we can choose what to believe moving forward. God lives in this space. In this space is where God communicates with our spirits.

Some spaces are so small that our response seems almost instantaneous. It's a snake - quick jump back! This can also happen in emotionally threatening situations. Your mother sends you an ad for a posture corrector with the message, "no one likes a hunchback." A small criticism can just as quickly trigger a defensive reaction. However, as we make the choice to question stressful thoughts, we have the potential to make that space larger so that we can be in control of our response. We become more in control because the truth has been revealed to us through the power of God within that space.

If the brain, especially the limbic system, labels what's right and wrong based on emotion and learned experiences, we can look for those same patterns in spiritual teachings. They are the spiritual stories influenced by this limbic mindset fixed on right and wrong. One example is the process of communing with God by way of two contrasting characters: the Devil and Jesus Christ.

Counterparts

We can learn a lot by studying the Adam and Eve narrative, whether you believe it as a literal event or a story meant to educate us on the human condition. Two humans are introduced to two counterparts. One who is sent to deceive and entrap (Satan) and the other to enlighten and save (Christ). Two clearly opposite persons with opposite goals. This is the traditional message. It is meant to illuminate the theme of good vs. evil. Right vs. wrong.

When Mother Eve was in the garden, God allowed the serpent of all stressful thoughts to come and "entice" Eve. How do I know they were all stressful thoughts? Because Satan is the father of all lies.[4] Yet, God still allowed this. He allowed this conversation, just as he allows it today in all his children. Why? Simply, we would not know truth otherwise. And to know truth is to know God.

Traditionally the Devil, Satan, Lucifer, the Ego, the Prince of Darkness, whatever you name him, is viewed as the enemy. He is taught to be feared and avoided. This does not compute with my heart. How are we to avoid something that is always there? And what good is it to fear him? He speaks lies to our spirit for our good, for our benefit. When we hear a stressful thought, we must have the courage to see it as a lie. Then, through the Atonement of Jesus Christ, we must ask if the

---

[4] Moses 4:4

thought is true. As we work in His Atonement, we will be shown what is true and what is false.

Changing the story of how we see the Devil will give us the power we need to act instead of being acted upon.

The Gift of the Devil

In the story of Adam and Eve, a threat comes into their peaceful garden to confuse and lead them to go against the clear command that God had given to them - to not eat from the tree of Knowledge of Good and Evil. Brilliant Eve realized, with this new presence in her life, that she needed this power to be able to distinguish between what was good and evil. It was the only way for personal progression.

This new presence in her life, the threat that encroached into their garden, was that of the Devil. Traditionally, he is illustrated as an enemy. He wants us to suffer. He wants us to fail. Despite that, the archaic meaning of Lucifer actually means a match struck by rubbing it on a rough surface.[5] Maybe we've gotten it all wrong when it comes to understanding his role in our lives? Consider that this dark presence is really designed to irritate for the purpose of bringing light (or understanding) to the person who is struck.

Threats to our spiritual well-being include stressful thoughts and feelings; also known as lies. This is where the Devil comes into play. Understanding the Devil's role in the process of

---

[5] "Lucifer: Definition of Lucifer by Oxford Dictionary on Lexico.com Also Meaning of Lucifer." *Lexico Dictionaries | English*, Lexico Dictionaries, 2020, www.lexico.com/en/definition/lucifer.

progression is the only way to uncover the truth that God wants us to see. We MUST be deceived with a lie to know we aren't living in truth. It's the only way. A lie must be examined and flipped around to get to the truth. This is the gift of the Devil. It is for our good, if we allow it to be. Otherwise, it will destroy us and imprison us as intended.

There have been many breakthrough moments in my life that have completely changed my entire reality. As I began my own personal search for peace of mind and answers to prayers, I started seeing this pattern: the thoughts that brought panic and depression in my life revealed the BIGGEST most groundbreaking discoveries. These accounts are real. They are intimate, personal discoveries. I share them in hopes that others may benefit and find peace in their lives the way I did. By understanding the Devil's actual role in God's grand plan, I found a way to freedom.

It is interesting to me that the word 'withstand' means to stand against, not with. Rightly so, to be able to stand against something you must stand with that thing - face that thing. "Resist the devil, and he will flee from you."[6] The origin of the word 'resist' means to "stop and stare." Therefore, the gift we have been given is the opportunity to stare into the eyes of the Devil in our minds. We must stop and stand with the thoughts that cause anger or sadness and so forth. The purpose of this is to discover the actual truth that is hidden on the other side of those dark thoughts. Once the opposite is revealed to you through quiet ponderings, earnest and honest searching, and sincere inquiry, all that will be left is truth, light,

[6] James 4:7
[7] "Resist: Definition of Resist by Oxford Dictionary on Lexico.com Also Meaning of Resist." *Lexico Dictionaries | English*, Lexico Dictionaries, 2020, www.lexico.com/en/definition/resist.

and peace. Thus, the Devil will flee from you as promised because light will replace the darkness.

Perhaps it's no coincidence that some circles seek the vision of the "Third Eye" (a symbol of spiritual enlightenment) to reveal truth to their souls. Just as the brain flips the image that the eye sees, painful or stressful thoughts can too be flipped upside down to reveal peaceful truths. This gift of the Devil makes it all possible.

The next step after utilizing the gift of the Devil is to work the Atonement that Christ has offered. But what does the word atonement mean and how do we use it?

The Atonement of Christ

Atonement, in a nutshell, is the process in which we are made free. It is the examination process of taking a thought that is not peaceful and uncovering the missing truth. In a very detailed talk given by Russell M. Nelson, the current president of the The Church of Jesus Christ of Latter-day Saints, he dissected the word atonement. In the Oxford dictionary, atonement is broken up as at-one-ment, meaning, at one with God. It is also influenced by the medieval Latin word, "adunamentum," meaning "unity" or "to unite." Other languages pair atonement with words such as expiation or reconciliation. Expiation means to atone for. Reconciliation has the latin roots of "re" meaning "again," "con" meaning "with" and "sella" meaning" "sit." Reconciliation therefore, literally means, "to sit again with." I am so in love with this definition of atonement. How intimate and special it is. One may only picture the sacrificial act that Christ performed on our behalf (dying to save us) when they hear the word atonement, but it conveys so much more when we understand its perfect and entire meaning. My most important goal for writing about Jesus Christ and His Atonement is so you may know for yourself how life-changing this perspective is in discovering truth for yourself and having that kind of relationship with God. He is a true friend to sit and talk things over with.

I imagine myself transcended into this plain white space. There are no walls, windows or doors, but there are no feelings of claustrophobia. I know it is an open space that expands into forever. I am sitting quietly with my eyes closed and hands folded gently in my lap, still as I ever can be. I'm sitting on a green velvet loveseat (don't ask me why, I don't even know) in the middle of this bright whiteness. I open my eyes and there is my Savior. Looking at me. I am not startled, because I had asked him to be there in my mind just moments before. I could feel him there. He smiles, not speaking, and I begin to pour my heart out to him. When I am in the state of atonement, this is where I go in my mind's eye. It may be different for you. I know that I become easily distracted, so I imagine this space when we are together; simple, white, and comfortable. I challenge you to create your own sacred space to sit with God again. Where is it that you go to sit together and work the Atonement? When we are in a state of atonement, we are being with God in every conversation. Our will is united with His. We want to see what He sees. We have sinned and wish to receive knowledge that may be hidden from us so that we can know the truth for ourselves. It's a beautiful and powerful state to be in when you are creating what the Atonement really means for you.

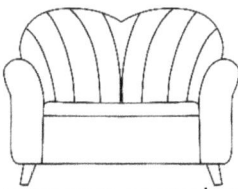

When I discovered this meaning for myself, I started to look at other words that I may be misunderstanding when it comes to spiritual freedom and working the atonement. As made obvious from studies done on the brain, we are meaning-making machines, justifyingly judgemental and limbic labelers. It's what we do. We are always looking to define things based on the way they make us feel. Specifically, there are words like atonement that mean multiple things to multiple people. Words like sin, repentance, and forgiveness have also been thrown around so often that they may feel empty or disempowering. They sure did for me. The word sin especially annoyed me. It was another thing I was taught to avoid at all cost. But, maybe I was getting this word all wrong too.

CHAPTER 2

"Meaningless Words"

What's the Word?

In this section, I urge you to take another look at the following words: Sin, Repentance, and Forgiveness, all words that may be familiar to those raised with a Christian perspective. These words have been spoken so often from the pulpit of my church it's as if they've become a part of the wallpaper. I recognized these words as they were spoken, but I didn't know what they truly meant. It was a process to uncover their origin.

When a word is first invented it has an intentional meaning, but over time it can become eroded, like a river eroding the walls of a canyon. It transforms and twists into many different meanings. The words listed above have been through similar transformations.

There are hundreds, maybe thousands, of talks and lectures that go into incredible detail about the meaning of these words. I could relate to many of the stories and definitions posed by some authors, but not all. Then something clicked. There is no meaning. These words are meaningless because they were understood only after they were personally experienced. In other words, a person put meaning to something *after* it happened. A person may not know true forgiveness until they have forgiven. Likewise, a person may not know what the Atonement was until they had experienced what it was like to use it. In every story I read, and every example that was shared, I realized there was first a story, then there was a meaning given by that person. Upon discovering that these words were meaningless to me, I realized that their definitions were mine to give. I didn't always feel this way. I've heard these words so often in my life that they frankly became like plain, white bread - bland, and not that great for you.

It's interesting how the overuse of a word can actually lead to loss of power behind its meaning, or even cause the definition to transform into something completely different. There was a time when the word 'literally' became popular to use within a comment. It would be used along the lines of, "I'm literally going to die," and the word 'literally' had its definition changed to mean something that was *not* literal. Amelia Bedelia would scoff at this notion. If you aren't aware of this loveable character, she is a maid by trade and does everything that she is asked; exactly how it's asked. You want her to stamp letters, she will put those letters on the floor and stamp on them with her feet until every one of them has a footprint. Gone are the Amelia Bedelia's of this world, literal is now also a term of exaggeration. The complete opposite of its definition.

Not only can definitions completely change, words that get used far too often may become less special or lose their impact all together. I had an extraordinary English Literature teacher in the 11th grade. She had once considered becoming a nun because it would mean she would be able to study constantly. However, she ended up choosing a more scholastic route, which concurrently satisfied the need she had as a college student to protest for change. She was a kooky hippie with long, red hair that hung past her backside with a passion for English I haven't seen matched. I remember one day she was writing on the whiteboard when she suddenly whipped her long hair around after hearing someone in the class utter the word, "awesome!" She announced her frustration with how we (the kids of that generation) had ruined the word 'awesome'. She romantically painted the picture of awesome as a word that meant, "to be completely full of awe at something." Imagine your mouth is open and the only sound to escape is the sound of "awe" because of the wonderment you are beholding. It would be like looking at the Grand Canyon for the first time. Magnificent, beautiful, captivating, inspiring. Over time its use was abused and it became nothing more than describing the feeling of your mom ordering pizza for weeknight dinner! She made me look at words a lot differently. This included the word sin.

Sin

One word in particular that I started to look at differently was the word sin. I understood sin to be, simply, any wrongful act. I was taught that some sins are worse than others, yet all dangerous nonetheless. Like 'awesome,' the word sin had been used so much in my life that its meaning morphed into how the word made me feel: fear and shame. The true meaning became lost to me.

When you look at the origins of the word sin, the word is actually multiple definitions rolled into one. In Hebrew there are different words that describe different degrees of sin. The words "ra" and "pesha" translate to the more serious degrees of sin. They are synonymous with words like "evil," and "rebel," and phrases like "to break away." The word 'traitor' comes to mind here. However, another word for sin, "chata," means "missed the mark."[8] I love this definition. I picture a dart board hanging in a game room. I'm aiming for the perfect bullseye, but don't quite hit it in my (many) attempts. In this way, the word "chata," seems to depict sin as the process of perfection. The continued desire to do and be everything our highest selves and God knows us to be, but finding ourselves falling short of that goal. One slight adjustment may be all you need to send that dart flying to the middle. Like the time I learned not to crowd the mushrooms in a frying pan from Julia Child. If you are sautéing mushrooms and put too many in the pan, they will not brown properly. If you crowd the mushrooms, you miss out on some decadent, caramelized flavors. Such a simple tweak makes all the difference. On the other hand, you may have applied all the tips, tricks, and tweaks needed, but still are unable to hit the mark. The problem may not be in your attempt, but by how you are seeing.

I imagine how hard it would be to hit the target if I wasn't wearing my glasses or contacts. Without them, lines are blurred and fuzzy. Hopefully, I don't hit an innocent bystander. No matter how hard I squint my eyes together, there's no way of hitting my mark. If the mark I am aiming for is, "loving one another", would I be able to hit it if I can't see myself loving them? Am I really loving someone fully if I say I forgive them, but feel a pit

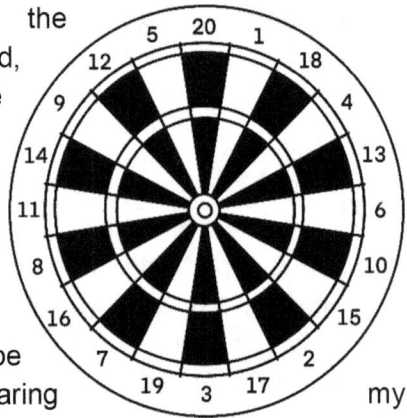

8 Heiss, Michael. "Hebrew Definition of Sin." *CBCG*, 2014, cbcg.org/franklin/Transcripts/Hebrew-Definition-of-Sin_11-15-14.pdf.

in my stomach when I am reminded of the pain I believe they caused me? Simply put, I can't hit what I can't see.

How does one see a target perfectly? Easy. You need the right prescription. The only way that this is possible is seeing with the lens of God (or Jesus Christ). For God sees only the truth.[9] When we are not aligned with God's truth, we are not at peace because we are going against our innate divinity. In other words, we are going against our highest self: the person that sees as God sees. The highest self is where the light of Christ dwells. Others may know it as the conscience. Regardless of its name, every man and woman was born with this light inside them. "That was the true Light, which lighteth every man that cometh into the world," so that they may recognize that light (truth) when it is revealed to them.[10] When we do not have the proper prescription, we are unable to see that light and, therefore, cannot see the truth. In that, we are sinning, or missing the mark.

It is not the sin that causes pain, but the natural consequence of not being able to see or feel the light of Christ within us. This happens because there is a stressful thought behind that sin (or action) that is hiding the truth. Pain comes from believing a thought that goes against our true nature.

For example, I was taught that it is wrong to lie. If you hit the side of your mom's minivan on a cement pillar at a gas station and rip off the decorative side plastic bumpers like an orange peel (true story), you don't tell her it was a hit and run. You tell her the truth. You tell the truth, not because you'll inevitably get into trouble, you tell the truth because it hurts to lie, and because the natural consequences of said lie are damaging.

---

[9] John 17:17
[10] John 1:9

When you lie, you become a prisoner to that lie. You constantly have to remember the story you told, because if one detail is different, it'll all fall to pieces. The belief you told yourself that led you to lie eventually becomes your identity. You adopt it into your life's narrative: "She'll never let me drive again if she finds out!"; "That pillar should not have been there!"; "It's never safe for me to make a mistake!" If I chose to lie, it is because I chose to believe those stressful thoughts. I am no longer free. I am trapped in a false story where I am no longer the higher-self heroine/hero, but a victim.

When we sin, we are believing a thought that causes pain, anxiety, or worry. In other words, we are believing a lie. If we did not believe it, we would not have sinned in the first place. We would not have sinned because our view would have been God's view: the truth.

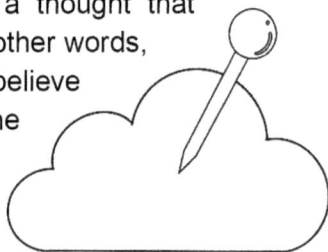

It may be important to clarify that a hurtful, sad, or stressful thought is not a sin. Thoughts move through our mind like clouds in the sky. Even the nuns in *The Sound of Music* know you cannot catch a cloud and pin it down. It is when we choose to believe a thought, that is not of God, that we "chata," or sin.

This outlook is not meant to condone sinning, nor point the finger at anyone who has ever believed a thought that caused themselves pain, and call them a "Sinner" (though I personally have come to embrace the sentiment). Growing up, though it was never said to me directly, I felt the essential message about sin was, "Sinners go to Hell." I believe this is a concept very much taught throughout many religions. However, what I came to realize for myself was that <u>"sinners" are in Hell already - Hell on earth.</u> To me, depression and anxiety attacks are as close to any Hell that I can imagine, and mine were all caused by believing a stressful thought so deeply that I saw no way out. Therefore, my new objective was to change the habit of labeling sin as "bad," or "wrong." Labeling sin in negative terms hindered me. It caused me to be stuck in shame and guilt, and became all I thought about. Instead of believing, "I sinned and I'm not good enough," I embraced the definition, "I missed the mark," and questioned the stressful thought of feeling 'good enough'. When I saw sin as 'missing the mark' instead, it put me in this space of hope. If I kept going, I would eventually be who I most desired to be: full of joy.

Words are empty and meaningless until they are not. Words have definitions, but an individual determines their impact (like an awesome canyon vs. an awesome pizza). The word "sin" does not have to be crippling. The meaning of sin can actually help you look forward to sinning because it's a way towards improvement. It's understanding that as imperfect humans we are bound to fall short. And that's the way of life! What if the concept of Satan's role in sin was not meant for our detriment, but for our benefit?

Sin is for me. <u>Sin became a quest of discovering truth vs. doing what's wrong.</u> I stopped avoiding sin, and embraced it instead. What's a more powerful place to be? "I sin and I am seeking for light and knowledge that God promised to send me," or, "I do not want to sin because it causes me pain." In the first, it acknowledges that sin happens. It's the process of perfecting oneself. It's so perfectly part of the process that without it, we cannot know the difference between what is false and what is true. There is no other way. The second statement may be accurate, but what happens next when you believe it? Unless we reconsider how we hold sin, it's Groundhog Day. We sin.

We're sad. We sin. We're sad. Over and over again. There is no growth in that.

If you choose to embrace sin as a stressful and unquestioned thought, then you may be ready for the next step in the atonement process. It is called repentance. Again, this action word was vastly misunderstood by me.

Repentance

If you have found yourself with the desire to unite your will with the father (or unite with the will of the higher-self), and utilize the Atonement of Jesus Christ that was given to you as a special gift and tool for seeking truth, you have simultaneously entered into the process of repentance.

Working the Atonement is repentance. Repentance is the process of changing perspectives. It is work! It can be a truly grueling process, like when a man named Alma *wrestled* with God over the frustration of people not listening to him.[11] It's not easy to challenge those thoughts that cause you pain. Even if you feel like they are a lie, the ego/natural man/Satan, will show copious amounts of evidence to keep you chained to that false belief forever. That is why repentance is a choice. It is a wrestling match between that ego and the higher-self to uncover the truth. When you are coming to God you are bringing with you the voice of the ego. These are the painful thoughts planted by Satan himself. Whisperings of inadequacy, doubt, fear, anger and more. As you present these thoughts to the Lord, your natural instinct (natural man) will be to defend them! Some are thoughts you've been holding on to your entire life. They made you who you are, and

---

[11] Alma 8:10

the natural man will fight to keep it that way. However, you made this choice to sit here with God and find the truth, as all men and women are free to choose liberty and eternal life or captivity and death.[12]

The paradox of this wrestling match is that the responses that come are gentle. They are an invitation from God to try on a new perspective. It doesn't feel pushy, like when the commission paid employee is inviting you to try on all these clothes you only kind of liked because you don't want to hurt her feelings, all while she hovers on the other side of the curtain. God's responses are gentle. His goal is to get you into a perspective that brings you comfort and makes you happy. When you find the truth, there is no mistaking it.

How can you describe the feeling that comes over you the moment an angelic answer is received? Especially one you've waited years for! It is like the saying in the Tao Te Ching, "The Tao that can be spoken is not the eternal Tao. The name that can be named is not the eternal name." When you feel it, you know. When you try to explain it, it fails to capture the real experience. I will tell you though that, for me, it is an emotional revelation. It's the "ah ha" moment that makes me cry, sometimes hard. To me, it's the moment when I feel the love of God. It's a tingle; it's a hug; or it's a clearing of the mind. It feels like a heavy weight being lifted off my shoulders followed by absolute quiet and stillness. Sometimes it completely devastates me, but in a way like a wrecking ball devastates a condemned house.

When you feel that love of God from the truth you discover, you have entered the realm of forgiveness. Dieter F. Uchtdorf, an apostle from the Church of Jesus Christ of Latter-Day

[12] 2 Nephi 2:27

Saints, has said that, "It is not repentance per se that saves man. It is the blood of Jesus Christ that saves us. It is not by our sincere and honest change of behavior alone that we are saved, but 'by grace that we are saved, after all we can do.'[13] His grace is what saves us. True repentance, however, is the condition required so that God's forgiveness can come into our lives." Repentance by itself is not what saves us from the Hell on earth that we endure. Freedom comes when we are forgiven for (innocently) living a lie, and that happens the moment we realize what the truth really is. That's when you enter into the state of forgiveness. Or, the state of being free.

Forgiveness

The root of the word forgive is the Latin "perdonare" (which is also the source of our English "pardon"). Perdonare is to give completely.[14] What is God giving to us in its fullness? A pardon, as in forgiving a debt? Absolutely, but could he be giving us something else? I feel that through forgiveness he is really giving us the fullness of truth, or the fullness of joy. Do you really want to be saved, or in other words, preserved as you are right now? With all the depressions, anxieties, and beliefs that bring you grief and sorrow? I do not. I sought this repentance from God for MY benefit. Not because of its necessity to get into a certain place in the afterlife, but that I may receive this fullness of truth and joy NOW - Heaven on earth. These powerful scriptures speak of this fullness:

---

[13] 2 Nephi 25:23
[14] "Forgive (v.)." *Index*, 2020, www.etymonline.com/word/forgive.

"And truth is knowledge of things as they are, and as they were, and as they are to come; The Spirit of truth is of God. I am the Spirit of truth, and John bore record of me, saying: He received a fulness of truth, yea, even of all truth; He that keepeth his commandments receiveth truth and light, until he is glorified in truth and knoweth all things. For man is spirit. The elements are eternal, and spirit and element, inseparably connected, receive a fulness of joy; And when separated, man cannot receive a fulness of joy."[15]

When we receive truth in its entirety, we receive a fullness of joy. In that fullness of joy, we know that we are forgiven and that we forgave the other person or thing that we saw had wronged us. This happens because we are not separated from God, but are seeing how He sees - the big/complete picture or even just another viewpoint.

Russell M. Nelson continued his discussion of defining atonement, "In Hebrew, the basic word for atonement is *kaphar,* a verb that means "to cover" or "to forgive." Closely related is the Aramaic and Arabic word *kafat,* meaning a close embrace"—no doubt related to the Egyptian ritual embrace." When you receive this "ah-ha" sensation of truth, you are embraced in this love that only the savior can express. Just as stated in the scriptures "the Lord hath redeemed my soul ... ; I have beheld his glory, and I am encircled about eternally in the arms of his love."[16] I hope that you are beginning to see the tremendous love that encompasses this sacred process with your Savior and your Heavenly Father.

On that note, how do we know we are forgiven, or have forgiven another after receiving this fullness? Byron Katie,

---

[15] The Doctrine and Covenants 93:24, 26, 28, 33, 34.
[16] 2 Nephi 1:15.

author and international public speaker who teaches a self-inquiry method known as "The Work," gives my favorite quote on the subject, "Forgiveness is the discovery that what you thought happened, didn't." It occurs in the process of the atonement when you are wrestling with God, and finding the opposite of what you believed was true. <u>Once you've discovered that your original thought was a lie all along, you have forgiven, and in turn are forgiven by God.</u> You've forgiven because there was actually nothing to forgive! It didn't happen. You've also been forgiven for having unloving feelings towards another person - they simply left. Byron Katie also said, "Forgiveness is just another name for freedom." There is true everlasting freedom when you are no longer a prisoner to the lies you've been holding on to. That isn't to say that factual events did not take place, just that what you believed about that event may not have happened as you previously thought.

When you are being forgiveness, you are saved. I say "being forgiveness" because it is something you are, not just something you do. In the past I have said in my heart that I have forgiven people but the bad feelings still remained. I wanted to forgive, but didn't have the faith that justice would be done unless I could always prove to God the amount of pain that person made me endure. It was when I actually worked this process of the atonement that I truly came to understand the freedom that comes from truly forgiving someone; and it had nothing to do with them.

Definitions to remember

Sin - Missing the mark. The process of perfection and source of pain.

Atonement - At one with God, to unite with God, and to sit with God again (over and over).

Repentance - The process of changing perspectives (working the atonement).

Forgiveness - Receiving a fullness of understanding. Seeing what couldn't be seen before.

CHAPTER 3

"How Does It Work?"

The Gift of the Devil: 5 Steps to Freedom

1. Sin/Source - Stopping to feel the pains of sin or the source of pain. You missed the mark and desire to be corrected. Pinpoint the painful thought/belief that's running through your mind. Focus on one stressful thought at a time to question.

2. Atonement/Sit with God again - Having the overall goal to align your perspective and understanding with God's. Having faith that this conversation will save you and free you. Where will you go to sit with God?

3. Repentance/Work - Dissecting all your pains, frustrations, and judgements that are causing distress. Looking to the opposite of what you originally thought to find the truth. Test out all different angles. I like to use Byron Katie's 'Judge Your Neighbor' Worksheet. You can find it at thework.com.

4. Forgiveness/Freedom - Letting the opposite thoughts sink in as truths are revealed to you in ways you never expected or thought possible - realizing you were wrong.

5. Repeat. For life.

Living the Process

Taking on these new definitions of atonement, sin, repentance, and forgiveness, may prove challenging to some. It takes courage to choose freedom. It takes courage to challenge beliefs that we feel are right, even if believing them doesn't bring peace. It takes courage to put down the things that numb us and distract us from pain (social media binging, excessive shopping, unhealthy eating, drugs, alcohol, sexually risky behavior, etc.) and instead turn to the pain to feel it fully and question it. Though it may be difficult, what follows is the greatest reward - true peace and real contentment. All the things I used to turn to for numbing me do not compare with the fullness of joy I receive when I choose to sit with God again. That's what keeps me coming back again and again.

This process is for us. It is for our good. Consider that the next time you make a "mistake" - it is all part of the process. It's only a mistake because you mistook something as truth. You would not have made the mistake in the first place if you were seeing with God's eyes. <u>The hint we get that we missed the mark is when we experience all the negative feelings associated with an action or situation. That is the gift of the Devil.</u> If we did not feel those negative feelings, we would not be able to know the truth that only God can give. The ego/the Devil is doing us a huge favor! We cannot become one with God, and our highest selves, without him.

To conclude with the words of Uchtdorf, "The Atonement of Jesus Christ is the gift of God to His children to correct and overcome the consequences of sin." [17] For God sent not his

---

[17] Uchtdorf, Dieter F. "Is There a Point of No Return?" *The Church of Jesus Christ of Latter-Day Saints*, 2007, www.churchofjesuschrist.org/study/new-era/2010/06/is-there-a-point-of-no-return?lang=eng.

Son into the world to condemn the world; but that the world ... might be saved"[18] Working the Atonement has saved my life. It has saved me from depression and anxiety that was destroying my happiness and crippling my ability to lead a beautiful existence. Through this process of understanding sin and working the Atonement, I have come to know true forgiveness and a fullness of joy. I hope that by sharing my personal experiences later in this book it will create the possibility of freedom from emotional pain in your own life.

'How-To'

Now that I have addressed the powerful process of using the gift of the Devil and the Atonement for receiving answers, insights, and divine truths, the question may still remain how do you actually work through this process? Or, after tapping into the higher-self, how does one see the truth from the lie that is being believed?

Hearing God's voice did not come easy to me. As a teenager I realized I desperately needed to learn this skill or I was always going to struggle. I still struggle, but I no longer see that as a bad thing. I'm growing and it's exciting. Joy comes about by suffering, which makes absolute sense. When we suffer, the answers that set us free were always there - they were merely veiled from our eyes. It's like living with blinders on. The removal of our blinders and this unveiling of truth is known as revelation.

Revelation is an uncovered truth that was once unknown. Revelations are answers given through a personal channel with God. They are proof that Jesus Christ and his Atonement

---

[18] John 3:17

<u>can enable God's children to create a world that obeys their every command.</u>[19] In other words, when we know how to work the atonement, revelation (revealed truth) changes how we see and experience the world. We become the authors of our life instead of believing that we are not in control of our life. If we command love in our world, we will see love. If we command hate, we will see hate, etc.

I feel like there is no 'one-size-fits-all' for working the atonement. However, there was indeed a 'how-to-work-the-atonement' for me. Crafting this practice took over 10 years (though its true origins started long before I could even understand what it was). I know it will continue to develop and morph as I go. The best way I can explain how I work the Atonement of Jesus Christ and the gift of the Devil is by sharing my own personal experiences that I have documented in my journals over the past decade.

<u>The majority of my "ah ha" moments (seeing where I missed the mark) came about through working on my relationships with others</u>, specifically, relationships with those whom I interacted most often and most intimately (my family, exes, and friends), though not exclusively. In 100% of the cases, it was me who was in the wrong, and it was me who needed to change (the complete opposite of what I originally thought). This is not to say that the other person is completely exonerated. It doesn't matter. What matters is that I want to be free and I can do that without making others wrong.

---

[19] Jacob 4

Be Willing to Be Wrong

According to accounts mentioned in the Bible, the ancient Jews were stubborn; seeking for things that they could not understand. "Wherefore, because of their blindness, which blindness came by looking beyond the mark, they failed; for God hath taken away his plainness from them, and delivered unto them many things which they cannot understand, because they desired it. And because they desired it God hath done it, that they may stumble and struggle."[20] A sign of stubbornness is the habit of talking AT God. It's having no desire to change one's self, but to complain and hope that is enough to change a certain circumstance. We miss the mark because we are not able to see where we went wrong, nor have we come to God with the purpose of discovering so. We claim we are being acted upon, instead of being the one that acted. Or, we argue that our reaction is credited to the fault of the other. To that end, we stake our claim as the victim.

Victims have been hurt and are not willing to see it any other way. A victim may still be able to feel the endless love of God, but they cannot receive the truth God has to offer because they are not willing to receive it, and will consequently remain in a stressful state. Like the painting *Jesus at the Door (Jesus Knocking at the Door)*, by Del Parson, it suggests that the Savior can only enter, if the person on the other side opens the door. Absent from the painting is a handle or door knob on the Savior's side, supporting this idea. <u>Victims only see that they were right because they had been wronged.</u> Opening the door takes humility. It takes looking at and considering how it could be you that was wrong (even if you were innocent).

---

[20] Jacob 4:14

Can You Feel the Love...?

In my experience, the truth is more invigorating than any painful or frustrating thought. When truth is revealed to you, you feel the lie in every way (mentally, spiritually, emotionally, etc.) being lifted from you. It's like the relief experienced after removing a 50lb hiking pack after the end of a long trek - finally feeling that breeze on the sweat strip from your spine and letting out a very audible "ahhh." If you don't hike, I've known purses and diaper bags to be just as cumbersome.

As I've been growing in understanding and the workings of the atonement in my life, I have slowly been peeling away all the stressful lies I have come to believe over the years. In these conversations with God, miracles have happened. Hearts have been changed, and lives transformed (mostly my own). Some lies take days for me to be shown where I missed the mark. Others have taken years. Working this process may be new for some. That's why it takes practice, bravery, and honesty.

Practice, Be Brave, Be Honest

Practice turning your thoughts around in small and simple ways. This year, especially, I have picked up momentum on receiving personal revelation because of this simple exercise. Often things pop in my head that compel me to say something to another person. Then, there is an inner voice that immediately follows, telling me not to say that thing. I think, "It's embarrassing," or "that person will think I'm weird," and finally, "How do I know it's from God, and not just me?"

Scriptures tell us that God lives within us: "And this I know, because the Lord hath said he dwelleth not in unholy temples, but in the hearts of the righteous doth he dwell; yea, and he has also said that the righteous shall sit down in his kingdom, to go no more out."[21] A life devoted to sitting with God means that he is not far from us at all. He lives in us; thus, any good thought that came to me, I knew came from him. Therefore, I stopped filtering myself when such thoughts arose. I said them, even if they were the most simple or silly things. If the thought came to compliment a woman on her blouse at Venezia's Pizza, I did it. If a girl wearing a Space Jam shirt was walking across the crosswalk and I thought, "I should sing her the theme song," I rolled down my window and sang it to her. If a thought said, "Ask that man if you can buy him dinner," I asked him (he wanted a burger, no onions). Because of this exercise, I have come to realize how close the Savior really is to me, and how easy receiving revelation from Him was after all.

Be brave. It takes courage to find evidence contrary to the things you think are causing you pain, and to find proof instead that they are a benefit to you and for your good. It's in that moment that bad becomes good, sorrow becomes joy, and anxiousness becomes excitement. Mel Robbins, CNN commentator, television host, best selling author, and motivational speaker said this about fear, "Fear and excitement are the exact same physical state. Your heart races, you might sweat a little bit, you might feel tightening in your chest, you might feel a pit in your stomach. You have a surge of cortisol. It's basically the way that your body goes into a hyper-aware state because it's readying for action. Now, what's the difference between fear and excitement? Really simple. The only difference between fear and excitement is what your brain is doing as your body is all agitated." Your

---

[21] Alma 34:36

brain is what is interpreting what your body is doing. If you tell your brain that you are excited to do something (instead of fearful), your mind does not know the difference. If you are feeling fear and anxiety, have the courage to find proof that it is actually the opposite; believe that something is exciting rather than scary. It is 100% in your power to create the meaning. Be brave and see how something you are feeling anxious about can actually be good!

Lastly, be honest, so that things are seen as they really are. In Oprah Winfrey's Soul Series Interviews she asked *Loving What Is* author, Byron Katie, about suffering the loss of a loved one. Byron Katie answered, "was it really pain, or was it something else? Is it sadness, or is it love?" Such a simple, yet powerful question. Be honest about what you are really feeling in the moment. Perhaps we have always believed a feeling to be something it's not. Could that pain you feel after a broken heart be something more sacred than you once thought? When we are honest with what we are feeling, our lines with God will open and he will show us the truth of our feelings.

With that said, I am excited to share with you a few personal stories that have turned my life upside down in the best way. Because I questioned the things I always believed to be true, even though they only brought me pain, I was able to feel joy. I am so grateful for these revelations.

CHAPTER 4

"HELP!"

No Way This is Labor!

When I was in the home stretch of my pregnancy with my second child, I woke up before the sun to the all familiar feeling of constipation that I had experienced throughout my pregnancy (more TMI ahead). Not a problem. As I had done many times before, I waddled wide-legged to the kitchen for some prune juice, and planned to take a warm Epsom salt bath. As I made my way to the kids' bathroom (the only room with a tub), ice clinking the edges of my mug (because prune juice is gross any other way), I greeted my husband, Loren, at the small desk we put up against the wall adjacent to the bathroom. The light from the computer screen engulfed him in the dark, revealing his chestnut eyes piercing through saggy eyelids, still a little droopy from the night's sleep. Peeping out from below the desk was his blue, sparkly cast he was fitted for a few weeks prior after rupturing his Achilles tendon playing basketball. I reported my current state to him with a kiss on the cheek, as I had many times before. He showed his usual, yet sincere, sympathy, "I'm sorry babe," then continued clicking the keyboard as I stepped into the tub.

After experiencing the consequences of consuming two mugs full of prune juice and an Epsom bath, I felt some relief and shuffled back to bed to try and get another hour of sleep before taking my 7 year-old son to school. However, shortly after my head hit the pillow, I was right back up with even worse stomach pains than before. They became so bad, in fact, I was afraid my bowels were going to burst. I was about to send Loren out to the drugstore to get some MiraLAX, but he suggested trying the midwife first. It was 6:45 am when he called our midwife to ask her what we should do. It took her a few minutes to get back to us. When she did, my husband, via speakerphone, described my symptoms. I chimed in here and there, mostly in between screams. "It sounds like you're in labor, Emily," she concluded. I argued with her, "This doesn't feel like labor!" She wasn't convinced and told us to leave for the hospital now. Our angel neighbor came to take my son, Achilles, to school. I emerged from the bathroom, grunting with each step like some wild beast, took one step out the sliding glass door and told Loren, "I'm not going to make it," and rushed back into the bathroom. My husband called 911 for an ambulance. He was very calm, as always, but had a hard time remembering our address. Luckily the operator could fill in the blanks for him.

Now, it's important that you know that I still didn't believe I was in labor. I was convinced that my insides were exploding from some terminal bowel eruption syndrome and I was about to be split apart from the pressure. With my first labor I experienced gradual contractions that lasted roughly 17 hours. That's what I was expecting. To me, those sharp stabbing pains in my stomach couldn't possibly be labor. I was, after all, still 10 days away from my due date.

Eleven minutes later, the paramedics charged in. Per the suggestion of the 911 operator, I chose to wait in the tub. The very first thought that came to me when I heard them approaching was, "I'm saved!" A uniformed, red-headed man of great stature squared his shoulders to the doorway and stepped over the threshold carefully and slowly from carpet to tile. While on my hands and knees, he came close and crouched down to meet my gaze. I was trembling in pain. I turned my head to look at him, not even thinking about the fact that I was without bottoms, and whimpered, "It happened so fast." He told me if they were going to get me anywhere I'd have to get on the gurney before my next contraction. Before you could say, "alley-oop," I was out of the tub and rolling onto the gurney.

When another contraction came, the same paramedic tried to get me to stay calm. "Did you go to any birthing classes?" I bellowed, "Yes!" (even though I didn't) "but, I forgot everything!" I didn't do the classes, but I did listen to hypnobirthing recordings for 6 months straight every night prior to this day. I tried to remember the breathing techniques I learned, but just could not get into the space. I was truly terrified. The pain was overwhelming.

As they loaded me into the ambulance, Loren started his car and was about to jump in when a paramedic shouted, "You, wanna come with us?" He stuttered, but instinctively responded with a decisive, "Yes!" They responded, "Well, you have to come right now!" Loren obeyed. He grabbed his crutches that were leaning against the car, leaving the driver's door open, keys in the ignition, and car running, and slingshot himself into the front seat of the ambulance. Luckily, the same angel neighbor that took Achilles to school later saw Loren's car door open. She pulled into our driveway and attended to his abandoned car.

The "F" word was being spewed out from time to time, but not by me. It shot from the mouths of the paramedics who were trying and failing to get an IV into my arm. The incessant poking distracted me from the pain. The pain was...WHOA! I was inconsolable. We raced to the closest hospital, not the hospital originally planned. Ten minutes or so later, I was unloaded and wheeled down cream hospital hallways. I heard double doors mechanically smacking open and shut and increasing chatter as more and more nurses came to my side. I pleaded over and over with them to please, "Help me!" Meanwhile, Loren was skipping behind me on his crutches at speeds I didn't think possible for a cripple. He let me know that he was with me. I told him to please get me an epidural (not for my so-called "labor", but for the impending surgery that I was convinced I was being wheeled into). As we found our way into a delivery room, instead of an OR, one of the nurses finally convinced me that I was in labor. I was finally starting to see. As I stared into her dark chocolate eyes, I held onto her every word. My eyes anchored into hers, and I did not speak. She was my beacon of peace. I had planned this role for Loren, but my soul had chosen her. At that moment, she knew it and I knew it, and she stayed by my side.

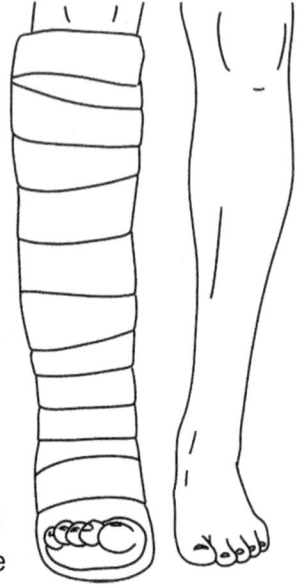

Suddenly, a doctor appeared as if he had dropped in from the sky. A contraction hit me and I screamed out in pain with my involuntary first push. The doctor, who reminded me an awful lot like the comedian, Louis C.K., looked up at me between my legs and sternly said, "Emily! Get a grip!" The whole room went still, like a classroom going silent after a student is reprimanded for misbehaving. "Stop wasting that oxygen with screams and give that oxygen to your baby! Now push your baby out on your next contraction!" It was the slap in the face I needed. I was quiet and focused. One big push later, baby's head was out. "Wait! Wait!" they all shouted..."Ok, now!." With the third and final push, baby was out! "What is it, Dad?" cried a nurse, for no one in the room, not even us, knew the gender. Loren in a tear-filled sputter, shouted, "It's a boy!," and then wept. Baby was born at 7:40am; 40 minutes from the 911 call to delivery room. He was perfect.

I'm not sure why I fought as hard as I did to remain in denial about my labor. Everyone else knew it. Heck, my firstborn also came 10 days early! You'd think I'd be able to connect the dots. I didn't. I couldn't. <u>I believed so deeply in another thought that it was my reality.</u> I believed my bowels were exploding and I was going to die.

Through this lens, I saw my rescuers and thought the phrase, "I'm saved!" In my time of grave concern, I longed for a savior. I felt completely unable to help myself, and I was right. I absolutely could not help myself in that state of being. Perhaps if I wasn't in a delusional state of denial I would have peacefully delivered my son in the tub, like those YouTube video home births. Nevertheless, that didn't happen. I was stuck in fear. Completely blinded by terror. It took multiple trained medical professionals to wake me up to the truth. The moment Dr. Louis C.K. (not his name) and nurses revealed the truth to me was the moment I was able to push Baby out.

I was fortunate enough to have trained medical professionals there to snap me out of the false belief that was causing me so much fear, and affecting my ability to deliver in peace. Though birth is imminent with a clear resolution, sometimes false beliefs and painful thoughts can be believed for years and years, without ever being released (or delivered) from the mind. Beliefs that in turn determine our reality.

When I look back, I see that:

1. Believing false thoughts to be truths caused spiritual suffering (fear, anxiety, etc.).

2. I saw evidence of the truth when I found the opposite of my original thought to be true (Yes, I could be in labor).

3. In that moment, I felt that I needed saving (Please, help me!); and they answered, "We will."

"PLEASE, HELP ME!"

I feel as though there is something to be said about the fact that I pleaded outside myself for help in a time when I felt the most helpless. My little baby relies completely and totally on me to live. I am his source for his survival. Left to his own devices, he would not survive. Even in a Jungle Book scenario, infant Mowgli is only able to survive because a wolf pack took him in and raised him as a cub. Over time we learn to feed, clothe, and protect ourselves; yet, there are times when that is no longer possible even in adulthood. Think of the hurricane survivors of the 2017 hurricanes Harvey in Texas and Irma in Florida. There are individuals and families who lost every earthly possession due to fierce flooding and wicked winds. According to CNBC, 80% of Harvey homeowners were without flood insurance and would not have the needed finances to rebuild. They would have to rely on others, including government programs, for help. If this is the case for our earthly experience, I'm convinced that the same can be said for our spiritual survival. Whom does one turn to when the spirit has been left destitute after a traumatic experience? Who is there to reach for when depressing and stressful thoughts flood and destroy the peace in our minds?

I am a spirit child to a Heavenly Father and Mother. Just as my earthly parents were the source of my physical creation and survival, my heavenly parents are the creators and keepers of my spiritual survival. This is not a physical discovery; it is a discovery of my heart that I know to be true. In the New Testament it states, "In this was manifested the love of God toward us, because that God sent his only begotten Son into the world, *that we might live through him."* [22] That our spirits may live because of him. I know this man as Jesus Christ, my Savior.

Some of you may not personally identify with Jesus Christ as the savior of souls. For some He may not even be a literal person. It could be an idea of the higher-self, or a connection to the Creator (whomever that may be for you) that you identify with. Please embrace that. I believe it is one in the same. The same thing can have many different names, so I hope you are not deterred by this name, "Jesus Christ and His Atonement." As a prophet has said, "For the Lord God giveth light unto the understanding; for He speaketh unto men according to their language, unto their understanding."[23] For me, Jesus Christ

---

[22] 1 John 4:9
[23] 2 Nephi 31:3

is the literal person I turn to for spiritual help, and because I learned how to work His Atonement (the process in which He saves), I can be free from spiritual suffering.

There are people on this earth with the desire to help heal hearts. People with the knowledge and know-how of overcoming mental blocks and emotional traumas. Search out these professionals in your quest for healing. Sometimes it's hard to see anything else except the trench you are stuck in. Those outside the trench with the right tools can rescue you. We are not alone.

As I sought for healing outside myself and went into myself for answers, I emerged with powerful discoveries. They have changed my world and my identity.

CHAPTER 5

"He Abused Me"

Trying to Do the Right Thing

When I was contemplating divorcing my first husband, I kept God in every conversation. I prayed, studied and searched tirelessly for the answer to whether or not I should stay married. I wanted to be happy, but I wasn't. I didn't know what I was supposed to do. I felt I had weighed every possible outcome, but remained frozen, unable to make a choice: true purgatory if I were to imagine such a place. A process fueled by the same belief: "I just want to do the right thing."

When I was 18 years old, I became pregnant with a child that would not survive. At my 12th week appointment, I learned that the baby had passed away. It would have been one thing if I had kept the pregnancy a secret; I could have endured the loss in private. But, as I was reaching completion of my first trimester, I felt the pressure to tell my parents. Even though we lived under the same roof, my father had spoken very little to me since I told him the news of my pregnancy. Even looking at me seemed painful for him. This was especially heartbreaking because of the immense love I have for my father - a father I had always experienced as being full of praise and deeply proud of me. His distance brought feelings of rejection, and in that time I developed the belief that love is something that is earned, given only when you are doing things "worthy" of love. Thus, I believed I was no longer deserving of his love because of what I had done. Evidence that supported my belief of being unworthy of love soon followed.

Some time after the news of my miscarriage, my father finally came to me. Sitting next to me on the edge of my bed, eyes to the floor, he broke his silence with this life-altering declaration:

> *"Emily, I want you to know the severity of what you have done. It is a sin next to murder."*

With tears filling his eyes he looked up at me and continued,

> *"I don't want to be in a heaven that doesn't have you in it."*

And with that, he collapsed his head into his hands and sobbed violently. He left my room some time after, and I was left alone with his message of fear. Based on the beliefs of my father, I currently wasn't worthy of heaven, and I believed him.

In fact, my father's words were all I could think about. He revealed to me that he had sought out counsel from a leader in our church to know what he should do regarding my "situation." That leader felt a great need to make it clear to my father the severity of my wrongdoing - the message he later relayed to me. I don't know if there was talk of redemption, forgiveness, love or second chances, but the fear had won in my father, and it had won in me. I believed that I was not worthy of love or acceptance unless I did the "right" thing. It became the lens through which I looked at life, and the evidence was everywhere.

As I looked around at my life, I noticed people I love start to pull away from me. I was labeled as a "bad girl," and I didn't belong with them anymore. This is what I believed; therefore, it is what I saw. I didn't want to be a "bad girl!" I didn't want to be pushed away. Therefore, this panic inside me grew, and with this pressure I was putting on myself to make things right, I ran to the only person I felt had not completely pulled away from me - the father of our miscarried child, and my high school boyfriend. I knew we could think of something to help get me out of my predicament.

The decision to be married was crafted while sitting at a metal table eating a Grand Slam breakfast at a Denny's Restaurant in Mesa, Arizona. When my boyfriend (we'll call him Rick) had proposed the idea, it felt like the morally "right" thing to do. It felt like it would be just the ticket back into good standing with those I believed I had disappointed. It would allow me back into my dad's heaven.

After the news of our plans to wed, it seemed family members started to emerge from the woodwork. More proof that this was, indeed, the right move. My choice to wed HAD to be the reason for their return, because that's the only way I could see it at the time. I was not interested in having a traditional wedding, but many of the family members insisted. I gave them a deadline of 3 days, and in 3 days we had a wedding.

I remember my mom pulling me aside right before the ceremony and telling me I didn't have to do this. There was no way I was going to let her ruin this story I had created for myself. I was angry she would even suggest such a thing. At that moment I had direct evidence contradicting my current belief that no one accepted me, but I was too blind to see it. Her words didn't support my current story. I wrote it off by telling myself, "Even now, she's displaying her blatant lack of support of me. If she really loved me, she would encourage my decision to marry." If only I could have seen her love for me then, I may have made a different choice.

In the world that I had created for myself, in order to get acceptance and praise (which to me was love) I had to live a certain way. I had to earn it. I had to be perceived as someone who was worthy to live in heaven with God, and that meant to be "sinless," and never make mistakes again, or at least not let anyone know about them. Therefore, every choice I made revolved around this rule I had created. The belief, "I'm trying to do the right thing," became my mantra. It became my religion. This belief, I thought, was a righteous desire to strive for. It took many years to realize that this belief was actually not of God at all. It was carefully camouflaged in a way to seem like it came from God, but in reality, it was as a wolf in sheep's clothing...leading me deceitfully down a road to 'Victimhood' - my new neighborhood.

The Victim

I was happy in my choice to marry. Not only would it prove to God and my family that I desired to make things right in my life and therefore earn their love and admiration, but also because Rick had proved to me that he loved me. He did not see me as a "bad girl", and I didn't see him as a "bad boy," even if everyone else did. It was us against the world. However, once the idea took root that I was no longer in control of my own happiness, I became a victim in my marriage. I became a victim to "doing what's right." As you may have guessed, basing your entire marriage on a foundation as weak as this is bound to fail.

A short time later the stresses of marriage took a toll on my husband and me. At 18 we had completely contrasting ideas about what marriage should look like. We never took the time to create our marriage together. I had been busy creating a marriage that I saw was the "right" way to be married. Similarly, my husband was drafting up his very own version, and it was not aligned with mine. My happiness became dependent on his cooperation of adopting my view of marriage as his own. When he was not cooperating in my mind, he was jeopardizing my goal of doing what was right. Needless to say, I was unhappy often.

The view I had of my world was weak and very limiting. I leaned on Rick far too much for my own happiness. If he was not accepting of me and my view on marriage or became angry or frustrated with me in any way, my well-being and self-worth tumbled. I felt betrayed. He was the only person who I thought accepted me. I believed if he truly loved me he would accept all of me, including my view on how marriage "should" be. The ironically heartbreaking thing about it all was witnessing him plead out to me, "accept me for who I am!" and I would not. I would not grant him this, even knowing how badly I wanted to be accepted. I couldn't accept the choices he was making. They went against my thinking of what a "good boy" should be, and I became the victim of it all.

The word victim is often paired with phrases like, "victim of circumstances" or a "victim of a crime." It gives this sense that it's not the person's fault, or that whatever happened was out of their hands. I felt victimized by Rick anytime he chose contrary to my marital vision. This notion soaked even deeper into my heart anytime Rick's choices resulted in serious naturally negative consequences. When I was being a victim, I felt powerless over his choices. I lived as though I did not have a say, because victims typically do not. Once I latched on to the word "abuse" to describe his offenses, my identity as a victim grew roots deep into my heart. It was an agonizingly painful way to be.

After our son was born, fear in me grew like a bad rash. I couldn't accept my husband for what he was doing, and I was worried about how his choices would impact Achilles. I spent two years of marriage ping-ponging back and forth between staying and going, afraid to make a choice because of my fear of needing to do the right thing. Neither option felt like the option that would grant me 100% acceptance from others or God.

Fear Not

The Church of Jesus Christ of Latter Day Saints have temples around the world. They are beautiful buildings, full of sacred symbols, and are meant to be places for quiet worship and a place to make promises with God. One afternoon, I found myself in the Houston Texas Temple looking for answers to the great debacle that was my marriage. I sat on an empty bench, alone, when I reached out for the scriptures, and started reading in Isaiah 54:

> "4 Fear not; for thou shalt not be ashamed: neither be thou confounded; for thou shalt not be put to shame: for thou shalt forget the shame of thy youth, and shalt not remember the reproach of thy widowhood any more.

5 For thy Maker is thine husband; the Lord of hosts is his name; and thy Redeemer the Holy One of Israel; The God of the whole earth shall he be called.

6 For the Lord hath called thee as a woman forsaken and grieved in spirit, and a wife of youth, when thou wast refused, saith thy God.

7 For a small moment have I forsaken thee; but with great mercies will I gather thee."

It was as though the clicking of a lock was heard and the door had opened. Never have I read a scripture that felt as though there should be a, "Dear Emily," written before it. I felt in my heart that God was speaking to me, telling me that if I wanted to divorce He would support me in that choice and continue loving me. Most importantly, what this scripture did for me was confirm the choice I had already made in my heart. I knew what I really wanted. I was just afraid to make the choice, afraid of letting everyone down (again), and afraid to break up a family for my own selfish reasons. I felt the scripture was God telling me to let go of the fear in my heart, make a choice, and move on with my life. God would be the husband in the family I wanted to create for me and my son, if that is what I wanted; and ultimately, it was what I wanted.

I did the best I knew how to do with the knowledge that I had. I really felt I was doing the right thing. I could see where I had fallen short, and I took full responsibility for the failed marriage. Nonetheless, deep down I felt that I had endured enough pain to justify my decision and that, based on what happened, no one else could possibly fault me. I was, afterall, the victim.

The Thief

After my divorce I was not finding the peace in my life that I thought would come from leaving a marriage I had deemed the reason for my unhappiness and distress. I was struggling fiercely with my self-worth. In my mind, I became a victim to the events that transpired during my marriage. I could not get the thoughts out of my head that he was the cause for all my sorrow. I saw him as an abuser who stole the things that I had considered my most precious gifts. He stole them! I believed he had taken advantage of my kind nature by making me do things I did not want to do. He used to tell me, "you can be happy in any situation." That statement made me crazy. When I go back there, in my mind's eye, to that time in my marriage with the perspective that I once had, I can be there again. I can be with the pain again. As I travel there now, I can see the thoughts that were hurting me the most:

1. *"I just want to do the right thing."*

2. *"Rick is a thief of my joy and takes advantage of me."*

3. *"Rick is forcing me to do what I do not want to do."*

I believed Rick was to blame for all of my sorrows. He was a thief who stole my voice (my ability to express myself), and I feared him tremendously for it. Whenever I got on the phone with him I would literally shake. My hands and voice trembled while I stumbled through a conversation. "He's abusing me again!" I would think to myself. Just seeing his name on a text message banner pinging on my phone sent me into a nervous frenzy. Not to mention, the way I tirelessly toiled over each text message and my response to any of his requests or questions was exhausting.

I saw him as <u>a thief who stole my son from me</u>. I was sick to my stomach every time he came to pick Achilles up for a visitation. I loved when Rick would go away in the summer for summer sales. I could have my son all to myself. Those longer stretches when Achilles would leave for a week or more were the hardest. It brought back all the feelings I felt in those moments in my marriage that caused the most pain, when I felt as though I was being forced to do anything against my will. That was my reality.

For me to keep up these beliefs, I had to keep giving them life. Satan never wanted these lies to die - that Rick is a thief, that he forced me to do what I didn't want to do, and for me to be happy, I needed to do the right things. These beliefs were all unbeknownst to me, for this is something I did not have the power to see at the time. All I could see was when I interacted with Rick, the result was pain. I concluded that he must be the problem. However, as the wise Stephen Covey, a principle centered educator and author of *7 Habits of Highly Effective People*, put it, "Every time you think the problem is 'out there,' that very thought is the problem." I did not see that it was 'I' causing 'ME' pain.

To keep these lies alive, and for me to be right about Rick's faults, I subconsciously trapped myself into situations that resulted in me giving away my virtue to other men with the belief attached: I'm not strong enough to say no. Thinking I wasn't strong enough to say no was the perfect cover-up that allowed the lie, "Rick is forcing me to do things against my will," to live on. If I felt I wasn't strong enough to stand up for myself and voice what I wanted, it was Rick's fault, not mine. Since I am a victim in all of this, I could not have reacted any other way. Satan, or the ego, is so good at preserving the lie. So good in fact, he even has these surface lies that you think are the reason for why you do things you don't want to do, but they never are the REAL reason.

The REAL Reason

Sleeping with other men outside marriage was against my personal values. Being racked with guilt over my continued betrayal of my higher-self post-divorce, I tried to think why I would do such things. Every thought I was given felt superficial. Thoughts like, "No one else is going to want me; I'm used goods," or simply, "I can't leave." They all felt superficial because when I looked at them, I didn't really even believe them; and yet, I was still going against what I really wanted. I continued searching for the reason for my inability to leave situations I wanted to escape from. My legs worked. My hands could grip and open a door. I didn't have a concussion, so I was completely capable of physically leaving, but I was stuck, held hostage by my own mind, and I didn't know why. All the while, it was because of this one underlying belief: Rick is a thief that steals my will to choose, and I have to prove it for the rest of my life. I didn't know that at the time. Truth be told, I didn't know it until I asked God to help me put it down in words for this book.

Since I also wasn't "doing the right thing" by disregarding my true desire to live a chaste lifestyle, I was a prisoner in a revolving door of sin, sadness, sin, sadness. It amazes me that a belief I thought was from God, was actually from Satan. I know this to be true because, in this context, living a life devoted to "doing the right thing" is a living hell. It's hell because it's a weak place to come from. It was weak because "doing the right thing" did not mean doing right by me and the truest desires of my heart (which were to save myself for a future marriage). It meant doing things to earn love and acceptance from other people. I wanted to never be judged or be the topic of someone else's gossip again. What an impossible and hopeless goal.

That was the most miserable time of my life and it was all Rick's fault- or so it seemed. In that time, God was lost to me. I couldn't hear him anymore; I was so engrossed with this lie I was living out as truth, that I was not interested in the actual truth that God had to offer. It wasn't until I had reached a point where I was tired of feeling miserable, that I was open to anything God had to offer. I was so tired of the depression, so tired of my codependency in relationships and so tired of sinning over and over. I felt the only way out would either be killing myself, or seeking help. Thankfully, I did seek help. I sought help because of an invitation, an invitation I hold in my heart as the most sacred and special.

"He STILL Calls You"

Achilles was now about 3 years old, and it was time for bed. That night I was prompted to read the scriptures to him. I thought to myself, "I may be a lost cause, but I don't want my boy to miss out on an opportunity to know God for himself, just because I can't." I opened randomly to these phrases:

"O ye workers of iniquity; ye that are puffed up in the vain things of the world, ye that have professed to have known the ways of righteousness nevertheless have gone astray, as sheep having no shepherd, notwithstanding a shepherd hath called after you and is still calling after you, but ye will not hearken unto his voice!

Behold, I say unto you, that the good shepherd doth call you; yea, and in his own name he doth call you, which is the name of Christ; and if ye will not hearken unto the voice of the good shepherd, to the name by which ye are called, behold, ye are not the sheep of the good shepherd.

And now if ye are not the sheep of the good shepherd, of what fold are ye? Behold, I say unto you, that the devil is your shepherd, and ye are of his fold; and now, who can deny this? Behold, I say unto you, whosoever denieth this is a liar and a child of the devil."[24]

Here was another "Dear Emily" moment, so perfectly packaged: "God has called for you and STILL calls after you!" I was being led by the Devil and his lies, by my own will and choice without realizing it. To hear that God had never stopped

---

[24] Alma 5:37-39

calling my name was obliterating. It destroyed the lie I had been believing that I was too far gone to be saved from my sin and depression. I was overwhelmed with the feeling of God's love and started to cry. Achilles was a little concerned and asked, "Mommy, why are you crying?," while holding my cheeks in his tiny toddler hands. I told him it was because I was happy. I hadn't felt happiness like that in a long time. Though it was only a glimpse, it renewed my hope.

"How-To"

I chose to start with the Addiction Recovery program that my church runs. It is very similar to an AA meeting, but with deeper religious and spiritual themes. I remember entering a classroom, not knowing at all what to expect. A circle of desks were before me and I chose the closest one to the door. Over the course of a few months, I attempted to work through the ARP steps. In my own words, these were the 12 steps:

Step 1: Honesty - Admit to yourself that you need God's help.

Step 2: Hope - That God's power and Atonement can make you whole and complete.

Step 3: Trust in God - Take on God's will as your own.

Step 4: Truth - Write down a fearless inventory of your wrongdoings.

Step 5: Confession - Talk about it with a church leader.

Step 6: Change of Heart - Allow the truth to change you.

Step 7: Humility - Be willing to see how you could be in the wrong.

Step 8: Seeking Forgiveness - Receive a fullness of truth and a desire to do better

Step 9: Restitution and Reconciliation - Make things right with those you may have harmed.

Step 10: Daily Accountability - Keep this process going. Consider a journal.

Step 11: Personal Revelation - Open your line to God.

Step 12: Service - Help others, touch hearts.

My greatest take-away from participating in ARP was the realization that within this program was virtually, and respectively, a how-to on working the Atonement of Jesus Christ. It took a concept that had been discussed so vigorously my whole life and offered an instruction manual on how to work it. I didn't finish the program in its entirety, because I didn't want the focus to be on my wrongdoings, but on how to get out of the old patterns of thought I didn't know I was in - my blindspots. Therefore, I started to branch out.

I wanted to learn how to actually work Christ's Atonement for myself. Doors opened for me like never before. I was introduced to other programs like Landmark Education and the 4 questions of Inquiry (The Work) by Byron Katie. These programs taught me how my life is mine to create. I can make any life that I want.

I remember one of the first things I did was call up Rick and tell him that I wanted to create the possibility of us being powerful co-parents to Achilles. I remember him being very leery of this, since my past behavior towards him had not been pleasant. He said that would be nice, and I became committed to living a life with that view: to stand together for our son, with respect and admiration toward each other.

This was no easy task as I was still, frankly, terrified of Rick. I was still committed to my beliefs that he was a thief and that it wasn't fair that I had to share my son with someone who did all those awful things to me. It wasn't until I went to Byron Katie's School for The Work, that I was able to truly forgive Rick.

"The Work" asks four questions:

1. Is it True (the stressful thought you are believing)? If you answer yes then you ask yourself,

2. Can you absolutely know that it's true? (Yes, or No)

3. How do you react when you believe the thought (the thought that is causing you pain or stress)?

4. Who would you be without the thought (or who would you be without your story)?

Then you turn around your original belief to the opposite. For example, "Rick is a thief" might become, "Rick is not a thief." Then I would ponder that statement to find any truths I may be missing.

To me, this entire process was working the atonement, and with this new-found knowledge I had acquired over the years, I got to work. I love this process because it takes those beliefs that cause suffering and allows you to see the opposite of that belief (the actual truth). Through this process I realized that Satan, and sin, is all for me. Without it, I wouldn't be able to see the truth - the truth of what actually happened. You can find more information about The Work from Byron Katie's website at www.thework.com.

Forgiving Rick

I had been resenting Rick for 6 years. I had told him, a few times, that I had forgiven him for the things he had done, and in turn, asked him to forgive me for my part in the divorce. I was sincere about my apology and took responsibility for ending the marriage and hurting him. I had used him for my own agenda, and that was very wrong of me. I realized that Rick had asked repeatedly for me to forgive him because he must have never truly felt like I had. He was right. I wanted to forgive him. I knew that if Christ's Atonement was real (which I truly believed), that it works for him, just as it works for me. Regardless, there was still a piece of me that felt like if I forgave Rick, and that pain was to leave me, it meant that what he did wasn't wrong. Forgiving him took courage. It took me seeing the truth.

The truth is: Rick did not abuse me. <u>I abused me. I abused myself by staying when I knew what he was doing hurt me.</u> I abused myself by allowing him to continue because I was so unconsciously committed to being the victim in the marriage. So, when it came time to leave, I believed I had an excuse great enough so that others would not fault me on it. The thoughts continued well after we divorced. In my mind, I was being abused on every phone call, text conversation, and face-to-face meeting when the truth was that I was completely safe. Nothing bad was happening. It scared my ego to state, "Rick didn't abuse me," because it had happened in the past! I was there! It was the cause of my pain for years! Then, I looked again at the image of the abuse and realized it happened one time, but I was inflicting that same mistreatment on myself every time we interacted. Call it PTSD if you will. That's what it was, but I was doing it to myself thinking that reliving that pain was making Rick pay! "Look how much pain I'm in, Rick! Look at what you've done to me! Justice!" Justice for whom, though? Not for me.

<u>I abused Rick. I used him to get married for my own selfish reasons.</u> I also used one event and treated him like he was lesser than me for years! Without the story that he abused me, I saw the truth. I saw Rick in a lot of pain, and I wept for him. I wept for the pain I had caused him. Because I realized the truth, I am able to live my life knowing that Rick is kind, and I find enormous amounts of evidence everyday. Incoming phone calls and text messages no longer set me into an anxious whirlwind. I am happy to hear from him because it means we are collaborating for better strategies to raise our beautiful boy together. I now look forward to hearing from him. Also, because my view of him changed (because I changed), Rick didn't feel disrespected any longer. Can you imagine what it would be like talking to someone who treated you like you were a monster? No wonder he was frustrated. When I saw him how he really was being, he simply was that. A man talking. The end.

I see now that it's not "forgive and forget." For one, you can't ever forget trauma. Just as you wouldn't be able to forget an injury - you have a forever scar as a reminder. However, you can be able to forgive and remember things a lot differently. Byron Katie says, "Forgiveness is realizing what you thought happened, didn't." I was finally able to forgive Rick because I saw the truth in the opposite. I saw truth in the lie. I thought Rick abused me, but he didn't. I was 100% responsible. So, there was nothing to forgive. <u>I was the one that needed to apologize.</u>

> This does not condone the behavior. It is choosing to see it another way. When the focus is on what's right and what's wrong, we miss out on an opportunity to be healed. When I take 100% responsibility for what happens in my life, miraculous changes take place.

That was only the beginning. Every issue that would come up, I questioned the thought behind it, knowing that it must be a lie (since it was stealing my peace). However, there still remained the thought of Rick being a thief, and it was most prominent whenever Achilles was being shared. Bringing this lie before the Lord to discover the actual truth was only possible because of one person, Loren, my new husband.

CHAPTER 6

"He's A Thief!"

Remember I had created the possibility with Rick of being powerful co-parents to our boy. It was easier said than done. Discovering the truth about my marriage to Rick allowed the space for me to feel comfortable around him again. I was no longer afraid of him, knowing that there was nothing to fear in the first place. I practiced being as present as possible with him on the phone, and really listened to what he was saying. Every time it was verified to me that there was no danger or threat present. Just a man speaking to a woman. However, a year or so after our divorce, Rick re-married. Rick and his new wife had a little baby boy together. This generated a desire in him to be with Achilles more often. This was devastating news to me. I did not like this idea AT ALL. I still believed, wholeheartedly, that it was completely unfair that I had to share my son with Rick. I felt that I shouldn't have to share Achilles with someone that had once hurt me the way Rick had! "It wasn't fair! He didn't deserve him!" This was the thought festering beneath the surface off my heart that I could not see causing all this hate and torture: "Rick is a thief, and he is stealing my son from me!"

I sang this victim song for a long time. It was painful anytime we discussed visitation. Rick's then wife did her best to help create a plan that I could feel comfortable with. She suggested a visitation schedule (because at this time, speaking with Rick about it got us nowhere) that gave Rick just a handful more days each month. She tried to ease me into the pool of visitation toe by toe. This made me even more flustered. Now I had two people to war with on this visitation issue. It was an extremely difficult process. I called my negotiation strategy, "This is what's best for our son," which I really truly believed. I believed he needed his Mom. He was still so little, and I feared it would be hard on him to be away from me.

The reality of it, though, was that I didn't know what was really best for Achilles. I do what I think is best, and that's all I can do. The truth really was, I was projecting my own fears onto Achilles. I feared it would be hard on me to be away from him. I needed him. Although I meant well and wanted what was best for him, the real name for my negotiation strategy was actually, "Rick, you don't deserve him." I truly deep down believed that and that belief stole my joy.

An impending visitation kept me awake at night, it made me hysterical at times to the extent I would cry uncontrollably, and it made the hate in my heart spread like wildfire. It wasn't until I met Loren and his sweet daughter that I would be able to be shown the lie I was living out.

A Blended Family

When I met Loren, one of the things I noticed right away was his untraditional relationship with his ex-wife, Carrie. They were so kind to each other. I was actually a little confused as to why they weren't still together if they got along so well. Not only that, but Carrie's other three kids with her current husband, Patch, would greet Loren in the sweetest way. Each time we walked through the door to pick up his daughter, Leah, for a visit, the kids would shout, "Daddy Warnen!" because that's what she called him when she was at her Mom's house, as to distinguish between her Dad and "Daddy Patch." I was blown away that this kind of world actually existed! What a strange and glorious planet I had discovered! This is what I had been creating in my head for the possibility of my own family, but I had never seen a real example of it before. It didn't stop there.

Carrie and Loren didn't really even have a parenting plan set up in court. I think I found the original copy once written on a single piece of paper in pen. My parenting plan had clauses in it with phrases like, "in the event of..." and numerous other hypotheticals embedded in the agreement. Overall, their agreement had stayed the same over the years. There were maybe a few tweaks here or there in their schedule, but it was never officially documented. Leah felt very central to their parenting time. Before she was in school, she called Daddy Loren anytime she wanted for an extra visit or to sleep over. She was free. I loved that! Loren would suggest an activity, and Carrie would say, "sounds fun," so easy-going like. There would be some Sundays that Leah would be over with her mom's entire family (grandma, grandpa, aunts, uncles, cousins) and we would come by to pick her up or just stop by to say hi. I had my son for many of these visits. Leah's Grandpa Paul would open the door with a huge smile and an even bigger, "Hello! Come on in! Are you hungry? Have some dinner!" We wouldn't get a chance to answer before he pulled out a chair and commanded me to sit down as they served us the dinner they shared as a family. I would think to myself, "This must be exactly what Heaven is like." One big family. No titles of "ex" this, "step" that; simply, family. We were family because in some way or another we were important to Leah. If we were important to Leah, and if Leah loved us, they loved us too. I had created this with Rick's family to an extent, but

Rick and his wife were uncomfortable with it in many ways and asked for many stipulations to be put in place when "his" family was involved. I respected that, but continued vigilantly to have relationships with all of them because they were important to my son, so they were important to me.

I was thrilled to see that they had ALL taken this vision on, and Leah thrived! She was and still is the most well-adjusted and happy little girl (or child of divorce) I have ever met. Truly. I wanted this for my son so badly, but I was still holding on to my story that Rick was a thief, and didn't deserve him. It was a scary idea for me to let go of all my reservations, and take this reality on 100%.

The Greatest Gift

I got a phone call one night from Rick telling me that Achilles was telling him about how we went over to Leah's grandparents house for dinner and he wanted all of us to go to dinner together sometime. Rick was confused, but curious about what had gone down. I told him about Loren and Carrie's relationship and I again hoped that we could one day eventually get to where they are. Rick thought that would be nice, but naturally was leery of the prospect. We were still so far from that place. Our conversations were still frustrating and rocky, but at least now we had hope that it was possible. Achilles made it possible.

One particularly hard day, I was borderline hysterical and stressed about a new pending visitation arrangement. I was sitting at our kitchen table crying to Loren about the heaviness in my heart. Loren became emotional himself and said to me that he understood the feelings I was feeling. He felt them in the beginning of his divorce as well. He experienced feelings of unfairness when his daughter went back to her mother at the end of a visitation and hated that feeling of being forced into this position of not being able to see his daughter everyday. It was triggered too when baby Leah would cry to go back to her Mom because she missed her. Then he shifted. I will never forget what he said to me. With tears in his eyes he said,

"Leah is the most precious gift that I have. To be able to share her with the world and with others brings me such joy."

At that moment, I was changed. Any thought I had of unfairness or pain softly left me. I was left with nothing but stillness and peace knowing that the words Loren was pouring out to me came from a higher place, a place I wanted to be.

In that moment, I could stand from Loren's shoulders and see a more excellent way - a way that allowed me to see the lie that was holding me back. I knew it was a lie, because it did not bring me peace. So, with God's help, I looked for the opposite. <u>Instead of believing Rick was a thief, I saw him as a person willing to share perfectly and equally</u>. I saw evidence of this in every phone call. I saw that <u>I was a thief, keeping Achilles from having a deeper relationship with his Dad.</u> Therefore, instead of saying no when Rick asked to take our son to something on "my time," I did the opposite.

Loren encouraged me to say yes in any moment I felt hesitation. Loren challenged me to, "Say, yes, to Rick's every request to see Achilles, just for now, and see what happens."

I did what Loren had urged. Any time Rick made a request outside our visitation time, I said, "Yes, of course." Even if it was a longer trip or just a dinner at his Grandma's house, I said, yes, as long as I didn't have any previous family arrangements or trips myself (which was rare anyway).

The more I said yes, the more peaceful the conversations became surrounding visitation agreements. I had feared that saying yes would mean that Rick would take advantage of me. Just the opposite happened. When Rick saw continually that I was willing to give him more time, he didn't fight to have more. He listened to things that were important to me, and I listened to him. Sometimes it didn't always work out and we had to go back to the drawing board. But the more I said yes, the more respect grew, until eventually, we created the perfect plan for all of us - a plan where Achilles is the center, and he has the ultimate say.

I pondered more on why sharing Achilles was so difficult for me. I had this thought, "I don't want to share my most precious gift with Rick." Then immediately the turnaround came, "I don't want to share ME with Rick." I cried even harder as the truth began to sink in, and I then made a powerful connection. Sex to me is a very sacred act, almost spiritual. When I give that part of myself with my full consent and desire, it's me giving my most vulnerable self to someone. It truly is a gift I give Loren. Then I thought about the sacred experience of giving birth, and carrying life inside me. Giving birth is a powerful symbol of Christ's sacrifice - water is broken, blood is spilt, incredible pain is endured, and sometimes a life is sacrificed. You see, my son - my greatest gift I can give the world - came from the same sacred place inside me. Rick and I created Achilles together. However, Rick has, in the past, hurt me deeply. As I thought of this I also thought, "If Rick didn't respect and care for me in our marriage, how will he be able to fully respect, love, and protect Achilles?" When Achilles leaves to see Rick, especially for these long vacations, I feel like it's against my will. I don't <u>want him to go. So, as he leaves, I feel those same feelings. I'm not giving my full consent,</u> so parting with him feels stressful. <u>I am continually abusing myself when I am not giving my full consent of the parenting plan.</u> The truth is, I knew I would never get less than 50/50, so there's nothing to fear. I needed to vocalize the true desires I had, and if it came to it, let a judge decide. No, problem!

It was hard to say yes to more visits for Rick, but because I said yes, when I felt that pull to say no, I was able to question the other lie that I kept telling myself. The lie is that Rick is forcing me to do what I don't want to do. I was able to look and see that I was being a victim again in my thinking, and it was limiting me to ask for what I truly wanted. So, without the story that Rick is making me do what I don't want to do, I was able to go back to Rick and tell him the things that I felt in my heart were in our son's best interests. Eventually, Rick and I had created the perfect plan for us, without any need to go to court. When stories aren't ruling the narrative, God can come in and speak to your heart what really is best and you can actually hear it.

Now when Achilles leaves me at any time (to visit his dad's family, to school, or even a friends house) I feel love, gratitude and joy in watching him leave, and I feel love, gratitude and joy upon his return. What a gift it is to be able to share your children with the world.

> John 3:16 "For God so loved the world, that he gave his only begotten Son."

Heaven is Here

The most important thing that came of all of this was the transformation I saw in Achilles. He has a sensitive spirit and was often overwhelmed, anxious, and easily frustrated. These traits only worsened when, at the age of four, he was in a car accident that left him with permanent nerve damage that affects movement in his left arm. Although he embraced his healing process with patience and enthusiasm, his ability to cope with stress had weakened considerably. In the past couple of years, as Rick and I were able to heal our relationship, Achilles has transformed into a much happier child. Things that once stressed him out were met with laughter and silliness. I remember when Loren and I were dating, he would get really mad at Loren for being too silly with him. Loren would joke with the kids and tell them stories about imaginative adventures like, he tickled a bear at the grocery store so he could buy honey. Leah would laugh and my 5 year-old would protest and scold Loren for lying to us. After some time, I noticed my sensitive son started to ease up and laugh along with us and now has many silly anecdotes of his own. When we had asked him what kind of parents we could be for him, he said for me to love him, for Daddy Rick to have fun with him, and for Daddy Loren to be silly with him. I love that creation we made together.

For Achilles's 7th birthday, Rick, Rick's wife, their son, Leah, Loren, and I, for the very first time all went out to dinner together to celebrate the amazing person that he is. It was such a happy reunion and one of my most treasured accomplishments. Not only that, but now we often have joint parties, and all family members from both sides come out to support his extra-curricular activities, competitions, and school or church events.

The greatest miracle of all is that even relative's of Leah's I have not yet met have been kind and welcoming. Everyone seems to have embraced this family dynamic we have created. It's just the way it is, and it's much too powerful to be swayed. It all started with 2 people making a choice to not let a divorce break up a family. In many ways, the divorce has created the biggest family on earth (at least it feels that way to me).

I'm so grateful to Carrie for the relationship we have created together. It's a very supportive relationship where we often brainstorm strategies for Leah to help her thrive. We are a team. Carrie also cuts my hair, helps me with my kids, and donates her chicken's extra eggs to us. She makes the process so smooth and effortless with her easy-going, fun-loving nature. I am beyond grateful for her Christlike kindness to me, from the first day we met. This all continues to work because of her constant generosity. I would do anything for her.

Now, it doesn't have to be this way for everyone, but it works for us. Our kids are happy, and no relationship is forced. It is as involved as anyone would like it to be. On the outside it may look strange to some, but it is true heaven to see all the people that love all of my children come support them regardless of title or background. It's a beautiful thing to behold to have a boundless family.

Reconcile

When Rick's marriage to his wife ultimately came to an unfortunate end, I had the urge to call her and reconcile with her. To echo again the teaching of Russell M. Nelson, *Reconciliation* comes from Latin roots *re,* meaning "again";

con, meaning "with"; and *sella,* meaning "seat." *Reconciliation,* therefore, literally means "to sit again with." Not only is it a time to sit with God and work the Atonement together, but it is a time to come back again to a state of togetherness. When I was angry with Rick's wife, I was separate from her. I saw her as an enemy, working with my once enemy as they contrived a way to take my son from me. As I realized the truth of who Rick was really being, I realized that on the same side of the quarter was his wife who I had also wrongly perceived. When I looked again, I saw her as an advocate for me, Achilles and for Rick. She spoke to Rick as a mother trying to help him see my side and my struggles of sharing our son. She was for me all along.

As immediate as the opposite thought revealing itself, a voice came to me and said, "Call her and apologize." I realized all the hurt I had caused her specifically. I imagined how difficult it must have been dealing with an emotionally frantic ex-wife and an emotionally angry husband, trying to act as a mediator between two storms. She got drenched. I knew that I must have played a very stressful role in her life and put a strain on their marriage. That being the case, I knew I needed to reconcile with her and apologize. I got on the phone, heart fluttering, and told her that I was truly sorry for causing stress in her marriage. It wasn't her job to be a mediator between us, and yet she took it on willingly to find a solution that worked best for all of us. I judged her harshly with thoughts that weren't true, and I was truly sorry for that as well.

On the other end of the phone call, I could hear her crying. I didn't know how she was going to react, and I can't speak for her, but I can imagine how validating it must have felt to finally feel like I saw her for who she was and understood her heartfelt intentions. I really did hurt her. I then listened as best and intently as I could to hear her side of the experience, and it was truly eye-opening. She described the amount of work she put into crafting out the perfect schedules of the constant negotiations, revisions, and details. She said she always tried to keep me in mind and help Rick see my side as a mother. Being a mother herself, she could empathize with me. She told me about the times when Rick and I were speaking on the phone, she would often have to put her hand on Rick's leg to calm him down when he was getting angry and remind him to stay calm, breath, and to speak kindly to me and really listen to me. I can totally see it too when I look back, because Rick would start talking in robotic, monotone phrases and say my name a lot. She was truly my guardian angel. It breaks my heart that I missed that for so long. I am so grateful for her, and for her coaching. It was such a gift to see her in her true nature - a nature I could not see because I was so blinded by my own false beliefs about her.

From then on, Rick's ex-wife and I have developed our own unique and special relationship. It seemed a pandora's box was opened, but only the good stuff came out. We talked and talked for hours at times. What I learned about her is that she is awesome! She is a passionate, creative, loving, and a fierce friend. She is generous and thoughtful, and is always willing/offering to help me. I knew that she would be in my life forever because we are the mothers of the brothers, but how wonderful to actually have her as a dear friend. Before I had my son, Woody, with Loren, she threw me a baby shower. That's right, my ex-husbands, ex-wife, threw me a baby shower. I took a trip with some close girl friends up to Sedona. A bit of a last hurrah, if you will, and she joined us. It was amazing to play and hike with her. We participate in the planning of the boys' birthday parties (she's the best at planning parties), and just enjoy each other. When Jesus spoke the words, "love your enemies," I thought it meant to love them in spite of "them". You believe that they are against you, but are they really? I never realized how much she actually rooted for me and cared about me until I met the real her. I truly love her.

Whenever I think that someone is vindictively using me or against me in any way, I challenge myself to see the opposite, to see how they are really FOR me. Maybe they are for me to teach me how not to be, or maybe they are for me to teach me how to be better. This is my world, my creation. How do you want to be? Hateful is not a feeling that I enjoy experiencing. It goes against my divine nature, which is to love all. If that is who I am being, God will show me the truth of that reality. If I am being hateful, Satan will gladly show the "truth" of that reality as well. So, who do you want to be?

I feel that there is a disconnect with many who believe in a distant heaven that they will get to go to when they die and have all of their problems be gone, and there will be no sorrows or trials. Does that mean our earthly existence is meant to be hell? To me, Heaven is here where I am. I may not be able to see it sometimes as I am foraging through the jungle that is my human condition, but when I work the Atonement of Jesus Christ I can return there anytime. What I do know, is when it comes to my family, the titles are nothing but, "that's my brother, that's my sister," and we are together because of love. With that view, my family continues to expand.

This wasn't always so. When Leah came into the picture I did struggle with a stressful thought that was making me feel distant from her. I didn't want to feel this way, so I did the work to change it.

CHAPTER 7

"I'm Not Needed"

Leah

In my experience, creating a functioning, happy, blended family is a delicate process. Figuring out that process triggered some very interesting beliefs for me. Stepmoms already have a bad rap thanks to Disney, but not knowing beforehand your role in another family can be like navigating through a mist of darkness. For one, I had never before dated anyone with kids. I didn't know what to really expect. Leah is Loren's only daughter. As I studied Loren and Leah's interactions together, I came to find a relationship with many similarities to the one my dad and I had when I was a little girl. It was loving, playful, and attentive. Loren is a doting father, and so much fun. I loved watching it, as many do not get to see that side of their partner before having kids together. It was also important for me to marry someone who would be a good father figure to my little boy, and Loren was just that. Figuring out my place in the mix, however, proved to be a little difficult for me.

Going from girlfriend to fiancé and finally to wife and stepmom brought up some interesting road bumps. Jealousy became a big problem for me. It was special when Leah came around, because Loren didn't always have her. He didn't work until she went to bed, and he always planned fun activities with her. When Leah was around, his focus was all on her. It made complete sense to me. However, as time went on, I began to feel like I was being pushed into the background anytime she arrived. I didn't feel needed or wanted. My jealousy came to a head when we took our first big trip together, without my son as a buffer.

Hawaii

After dating for some time, we took a trip to Oahu to visit Loren's sister, and I quickly dubbed myself the 3rd wheel of the trip. One afternoon, waiting for Loren's sister to join us for lunch, I remember grabbing for Loren's hand while we were participating in one of Leah's favorite activities - shopping. We walked inside an H&M, and as soon as our hands met, he just as quickly shook his grip loose and ran to Leah's side. I felt left out and just held my own hand. I remember that night calling my mom when I had a minute alone and crying to her. I felt so unwanted and uncomfortable being there. I was considering flying home. It was the first time I really resented their relationship. My mom told me I should tell Loren how I was feeling. After a not-so-restful night's sleep, I did end up talking about it with Loren the next morning, and he did feel bad that I felt that way. He said that he wanted to make sure Leah's first time to Hawaii was special and memorable. I told him that this was also our first time in Hawaii together, and I was hoping it would be special for us, too. After we spoke, he showed a definite improvement and the rest of the trip I felt included and considered. Nevertheless, I never moved on from those feelings of loneliness. A belief had formed, and that was, "Loren will always love Leah more than me," and the evidence began showing up more and more. I started to dread days we would pick her up to spend time with her because I knew it would be, "Leah time." Those feelings from Hawaii would resurface, and the pain of jealousy would be felt all over again.

Mexico

A couple of months before Woody arrived, Loren and I took a babymoon to Mexico for a couple of days to just relax and be together. We had a really fun drive. We laughed, listened to music and listened to books and discussed them. The subject shifted to Leah. In the past, this had been a very touchy subject, as Loren is very protective of Leah. I told him again about my feelings during the Hawaii trip, and he was surprised that it still bothered me. I told him the blocks that I was having towards Leah. Even after 2 years of marriage, it still felt like we had two family units; my son and I, and Leah and Loren. Then, I shared something with him I didn't realize was within me. Growing up, I didn't feel very close to my mom. I got everything I needed from my dad - appreciation, affection, love, adoration, encouragement, conversation, and friendship. Therefore, I had this underlying belief that since Loren was enough for Leah, she didn't need me. Loren felt that disconnect, and apparently so did Leah. He told me that she had expressed to him that she felt a lack of attention and love from me. Loren had been concerned about this. He wanted to speak to me on her behalf and figure out why I wasn't giving this to her. One thing I could think of was how unnatural it felt to me to mother Leah the way I do my son. It's not that I didn't love Leah. She is loveable, hilarious, and more easy-going than any child I have ever met. I just felt this awkwardness, confused why she would even seek out more from me. Plus, there was this pressure I felt from Loren to give Leah more of myself than I knew how to give. It really all boiled down to this one thought; "I'm not needed." Leah doesn't need me. I felt like my son needed me. For one, he needs a caregiver and a teacher. As his primary caregiver, he has always relied on my consistency in his life, especially since his Dad had a job (at the time) that took him away for months at a time. I felt very responsible for him. On the other hand, Leah doesn't need anything from me when she has her father around. She gets what she needs from him, and when she's not with him, her mom takes care of her.

Psychiatrist and adjunct professor emeritus in the Department of Psychiatry and Behavioral Sciences at the Stanford University School of Medicine and the author of the bestselling books *Feeling Good: The New Mood Therapy*, David D. Burns often poses his questions around stressful thoughts in this way: "What is awesome and positive about this stressful belief that you have?" He challenges his clients to take a feeling that is negative and see why it's actually a good thing. What I want to teach my children is that they don't need me to have a wonderful and fulfilling life. If anything were to happen to me, I hope that they know they can be strong without me. However, the thought, "I'm not needed," did not feel awesome and positive. It felt isolating and unloving. So, I knew I needed a different perspective.

Now, in the past Loren struggled to have this conversation with me. It was hard for him to hear that I was having these issues connecting with Leah. This time, however, he shared that he could see times where he had doted on Leah and gave her affection, but chose not to give me any. He also could see times where he was more patient and spoke kinder to Leah, but not to me. He said it was tough for him because his ego told him in this situation, "Sorry Leah, let's go. She doesn't love you. We tried!" He continued, "I know this must have been really scary for you to share with me." I popped back, "Yes,

TERRIFYING because of how much I knew that's where your thoughts go - to leave me and take Leah with you!" He apologized and said that he would work on being better.

When we arrived at our condo in Rocky Point, Loren sat down next to me at the kitchen table, looked at me and said,

> "Emily, your true nature is to love unconditionally. I've seen the way you treat everyone you meet — without judgement, story, or negative view — always with unconditional compassion. When I see the way you are being with Leah, I know that there is a block there for you. I have a better idea who I need to be for you so that you feel supported, but when you aren't loving Leah unconditionally, you are going against who you really are. Love Leah without a story."

When Loren got that inspiration from God on my behalf, it sent chills everywhere. Loren may have been speaking on Leah's behalf earlier, but my Heavenly Father was speaking to Loren on my behalf now. I've never felt more in tune with the Father/Daughter relationship than in that moment. I could see in that moment that the responsibility he felt toward Leah was the same responsibility God felt for me.

Creating a Stepmom For Leah

Loren continued telling me to create the kind of relationship I wanted with Leah from a place of unconditional love, and he would support whatever I created. Before, I took such a passive stance with Leah. She moved - I moved. Whatever she wanted from me, I gave to her. If she grabbed my hand, I would hold onto hers. If she wanted to sit next to me, I would make room. When I found out that she wanted more from me, my stories held me back from being able to even know the kind of connection I wanted to make with her. I am extremely lucky to have a stepdaughter who actually likes me, wants to be around me, and doesn't see me as Maleficent or Lady Tremaine. I know that there are numerous stepmothers who try to be close with their stepdaughters, but are met with rejection. Leah has always been welcoming, loving, and accepting of me. It's probably a big reason why Loren made the leap to ask me to marry him. Leah was rooting for me.

With this discovery, I made a list of who I want to be for Leah. Here's what I came up with:

1. Someone she can come to when she's struggling or looking for advice. Someone safe to talk to - a friend.

2. A hand to hold and a body to cuddle with.

3. An advocate for and protector of her.

4. A teacher of how to be happy in life, and how to respect and love yourself.

5. Someone to laugh hard with and be silly with.

I created the possibility of loving Leah unconditionally and without a story. I'm a powerful example of loving others without a story so that all my children can stand from my shoulders and see a more excellent view of what a life full of love looks like.

I always did this special bedtime routine with my son since he was a baby. I read to him, sang to him, and chatted with him before bed and always let him tell me one more thing before walking out the door. Loren had a special routine with Leah that also included reading and a nice wind-down sleep meditation that she loves. Before, I would just go into her room, give her a hug and a kiss and quickly scamper out. However, knowing that she has a special interest in music and the arts, I told her that on the nights she sleeps at our house I would read her a famous poem and then discuss it. I told her that whether she wants to write music or paint great art, poetry will be a great start, and it can be just our thing. It's something really special we share. Another benefit of creating opportunities to be silly with Leah is being able to be silly with her and her other siblings on her mom's side. Recently I went over there, got jumped on and we played with snapchat features on my phone. They flipped out over all my ridiculous kaleidoscope face angles. As a stepmom to Leah, I teach Achilles to protect her and stand up for her if she's ever in trouble or needs a friend. I tell him that he is a protector of women. And of course, I now look for chances to come to her for hugs and cuddles.

I Am Needed

It wasn't the belief, "Loren loves Leah more than me," that caused my feelings of loneliness like I originally thought. I couldn't prove that to be true anyways. Nor did I believe that I needed Loren to love me more than Leah. When I saw him leaving me for Leah that day at H&M, it exposed a hurt in me that I didn't even know I had. I realized that I felt closer to my dad more than my mom. That was really hard to admit to myself. <u>There was a lot of hurt there that I was projecting onto Leah and Loren's relationship because I had resentments towards my own mother.</u> Because I didn't create a unique relationship with Leah in the beginning, I fell back on the example of my perceived relationship with my mother from when I was Leah's age. That is what was painful. It had nothing to do with Leah. Believing that Leah doesn't need me like she needs Loren was the reason I isolated myself from them. When they were together, I made an effort to look for all the ways I was the third wheel. The truth is I am needed. I am needed because I have the potential to be a great influence on Leah. The question is: what kind of influence? Influencer of strength? Then I must be strong. Influencer of confidence? Then I must be brave. Influencer of love? Then I must be vulnerable. I want to be close with her. I want to love her unconditionally, and I need to have clarity to be able to do so. To do this, I needed to forgive my mom.

CHAPTER 8

"She's Not My Friend"

Lunch With Phoebe

One of my focuses for the 2017 new year was to become closer with my younger sister, Phoebe. We are roughly 8 years apart. That year she was attending ASU and living in an apartment close to the Tempe campus. I began with a simple weekly call or text, asking her how her week had gone and how school was going. I thought I had a good relationship with all my siblings, but truth be told I didn't know them very well at all.

For Phoebe's birthday, I invited her out to lunch on Mill Avenue, close to campus, at one of my favorite pizza spots. It had been a while since I had seen her, and I jumped at the chance to talk in person. Plus, who would turn down free food?! She arrived sporting her maroon ASU cap and a relaxed, natural, makeup-free look. She is still gorgeous.

Lunch conversation was off to a slow start, almost blind date bad - short answers, cushioned by long periods of awkward silences, until I could pull another topic out of the air. After some small talk, I finally asked Phoebe something that had been on my mind,

"Where do you think it all went wrong with Dad and you?"

Apparently, I hit a nerve. Phoebe had plenty to say on that subject. The reason I brought up the question was because I'd noticed that in that past year, Phoebe's relationship with our dad had become incredibly strained and distant. So bad, in fact, that my dad didn't even have her current address or new phone number. I knew it had a lot to do with the events that had transpired after my father remarried. Since the marriage, Phoebe felt that she had lost a lot of Dad's support. There were changes that were made that she completely disagreed with. That was only the tip of the iceberg, of course. She had struggled feeling close with him for most of her life. Her answer to my question surprised me. She said,

"Oh, I think he's always been this way."

That grabbed my attention. She proceeded to talk and talk. It's probably the longest I had ever talked to her in my entire life. At that time, her opinion of Dad was not very good. The more I listened to her, the more I realized that we grew up with a completely different view on Dad.

Different Parents

I always felt close to my dad. We have a very special connection. As a child, I ate up everything he said, as if God himself were saying it. He was my coach in sports, brought me flowers after my dance recitals, encouraged my writing, and always told me how beautiful and wonderful I was. Phoebe had a very different opinion of Dad. She didn't feel like he was very interested in her or her life. She also felt angry by the way he had treated our Mom in their 20-year marriage. I knew what she was referring to, but I wasn't mad at my dad at all. I forgave him easily.

While Phoebe was busy being mad at Dad, my anger was directed toward our mom. Years before, on the front porch of our newest rental house, my newly-divorced mother and I sat side by side on a small wooden bench. It was there she had expressed to me her heartfelt fears about the family blaming her for the divorce. She then told me all of my dad's transgressions. I told her that we don't blame anyone, and I begged her not to tell the other siblings what she told me. She did anyway. I was angry at her, I felt she was trying to make my dad look bad. I felt the things she said were none of our business anyways. Deep down, I simply didn't want to hear it. I hated knowing.

I quickly realized that it wasn't just Dad who we saw so differently, but our mom as well. It seemed as though we were being raised by completely different parents. Phoebe continued to talk about Mom. She said that growing up she noticed the times when Mom seemed sad when no one else did. She didn't understand it at the time, but being older she now recognized the struggles our mother endured. Sometimes when Mom would come home from work, she would sit in her car for 5-10 minutes looking at her phone before coming in. This was before Facebook or Instagram, or even the internet in general on phones, so what she looked at for 10 minutes, I'll never know. I remember this distinctly, and was very annoyed that after being away from us for so long, she wouldn't hurry up and come inside! I was hungry! I never thought about it really other than one of those Mom quirks she had. Phoebe on the other hand knew better. She saw how mom was sitting in her car, dreading coming into the house to play "housekeeper" after working all day. Phoebe said she wished the rest of us kids were nicer to her. The next thing Phoebe said had me paralyzed. She explained to me that ever since she could remember, she had the desire to be Mom's friend. Not only that, but she wanted to be Mom's best friend, especially since no one else wanted to.

Her words affected me deeply, like a knife to the heart, twisting every which way. Phoebe noticed that on weekends, Dad would do whatever he could to avoid Mom and work outside the house as much as possible. When she talked to Mom about it, Mom said she didn't understand why Dad didn't want to be around her, hang out with her, or get to know her. Phoebe felt Dad was completely in the wrong. She believed Mom was and is the COOLEST person. Everywhere she went, men and women who knew our Mom would stop us on the street and praise her and tell us the greatest things about her. Phoebe absolutely agreed with them. We saw our Mom completely differently, indeed.

When I was growing up, I'd see my Dad working in the yard. I would love to go jump on his lap and ride the lawn mower with him while he cut the grass (this was back in Georgia - where grass comes from). Eventually, the rumbling of the mower would lull me to sleep. I didn't blame him for not wanting to be around Mom, I didn't want to be around her either. In my mind, she was angry, anxious, and paranoid. It was difficult for me to remember even a handful of pleasant interactions with her. Phoebe knew that wasn't the REAL Mom. The real mom was the person other people saw. The stress of parenthood and feelings of rejection just got in the way.

I did not want to be close with my mom growing up. I felt like she never trusted me, so I never talked to her about anything, which made her even more angry and paranoid towards me, which then made me not want to be around her all the more. Phoebe was wiser. She knew that Mom was only being that way because I was being secretive. She had endured the secrecy for the majority of her marriage to Dad, knowing there was something he was hiding from her but uncertain what it could be. All these events that I could perfectly recount, Phoebe experienced them in a completely opposite way.

Not Your Friend

There were a few times growing up when my mom said a common phrase. I'm sure other kids have heard their parents say:

> *"I'm not your friend, I'm your parent. You have enough friends to tell you what you want to hear. I'm here to tell you the truth."*

As a young woman, I responded to that statement in a sort of, "Fine, screw you then," mentality. I told Phoebe that was exactly why I didn't want anything to do with Mom. Phoebe responded,

> *"Yeah, you were just like Dad."*

My jaw dropped. I didn't know what to say. It was true. In that instant my world changed. Irrevocably, I saw that I had sided with my dad on EVERYTHING. I did not like the person my mom was. I didn't want to be around someone who was sad and angry all the time. Thus, everything my mom said or did, I made it fit the story I already had of her.

Phoebe, on the other hand, had a beautiful story of our mom. She saw my mom as someone who had been really hurt and so had hidden her real self from our family. But Phoebe knew she was in there, and she would look for anything that supported her story of our mom. Phoebe loved my mom unconditionally. When no one else wanted to be close to her - she drew closer. When my mom would spout her "I'm not your friend speech," Phoebe didn't care. She only pushed harder to be her friend. She knew the person my mom really was. Someone who was wonderful, kind, generous, and funny, and her mission was to reveal that person.

Whenever Phoebe got the chance to talk to my mom about her day, she told her everything. She told her who her friends were, what boy she liked, what boy she didn't like and what she thought about things. She was never afraid to be detailed or even tell my mom things she tried or did. Phoebe had created this possibility of revealing the real Mom by being someone who revealed everything about herself. She opened herself up completely to Mom, regardless if it made her look good or not. In return, Mom did the same. She's told her things I've never heard before. I remember when I had told my mom about the real reasons I was divorcing Rick, she would tell me these incredibly personal stories I had never heard before. I remember walking around thinking, "Why didn't she tell me these things sooner?! I would have avoided all this heartache if she would have been more open towards me growing up!'" Then I realized how wrong I was. It was almost as if I was putting some of the blame on her for my divorce, like the pain could have been avoided if it weren't for her keeping these lessons from me. Then it hit me. It had never been clearer to me in that moment how entitled I was being. Because she was my mother, I felt entitled to her secrets, to her life. I felt like it was owed to me without doing anything in return. Yet, here I am being secretive and closed off to her, angry that she would be closed off to me. It's incredible how backwards that thinking was.

So, here I am at lunch with my younger sister Phoebe, thinking so haughtily that I'm going to help her repair her relationship with Dad, when it was me who needed the repairs. I was convinced that I had forgiven my mother for all the things I had resented her for over the years. I even apologized to her for having these resentments years before. It went like this.

About 5 years before this meeting with Phoebe, I came home late one night when Achilles and I were living with my mom. I jumped on her bed at 10:00pm, and woke her up to tell her how sorry I was for holding these bad feelings against her for so many years. I was sincere. The next morning she had written me a note and pushed it under my bedroom door. It said, "I don't know what just happened, all I can say is 'Did that just happen?' My prayers have been answered!" It felt so good. As the years went by, we were closer than ever before. I saw the real mom that Phoebe had known all these years. She is the most generous and wonderful person I know. Nevertheless, there was still something irking in the back of my mind, a feeling that things would have been different for me if only my mom had been different with me as a kid. I still wasn't that close with her as far as telling her how I lived my life or what I was thinking or feeling. I was afraid of how she would think of me. Even when I was dating, I only told her parts of my relationship and hid the rest away. It seemed my forgiveness was only partial, even though I truly desired to let the past go completely and move on.

When I left lunch with Phoebe, I thanked her for this conversation that had truly changed my entire perspective. It truly was transformative. I got back in my car and called Loren to tell him what I had said. I cried and cried to him. I honestly didn't stop crying for days. I cried at the courage and love my sister had when my mom made it clear she didn't want to be friends and she was her friend anyway. I was in awe how Phoebe could look beyond my mom's mood swings, not taking it personal, only wanting to love her more. I realized in that moment what my true self had always wanted. What I really wanted most was to be my mom's friend, too. It rang so true in my heart. I've wanted that secretly for so long, even though I didn't think it was really possible. I had forgiven my mom and things were great between us, but deep down the little girl in me still had this certain view of her. It wasn't until my lunch with Phoebe that I realized it was me in the wrong the entire time. It was I who chose not to have a relationship with my mom. And I found plenty of evidence to justify that choice. All the while, Phoebe saw the exact same things and drew opposite conclusions. She wanted to be friends with my mom, so she was. Their relationship wasn't perfect, but it was consistent and based on a beautiful value - vulnerability.

Friends

For the first time in my life, I tried on those lenses. What would it look like if I were friends with my mom? I texted her that afternoon after lunch with Phoebe and invited her to dinner, my treat. She was so excited! I came to dinner with one goal in mind: understand my mom. I asked her everything and anything I could think of that I wanted clarifying. We talked for more than 3 hours. As we were walking out, the parking lot speckled with only a few cars, she and I continued on and on. I probably would have lingered longer if it wasn't for Woody having a blowout and Loren texting me, asking if I was alive. I finally got my friend I had longed for. And she is truly one of the greatest people I know. When I see my mom now, I'm excited to see her! I think, "Oh yay, Mom's here!" I want to tell her things and be close to her.

Perspective is everything. You put meaning to everything that happens in your life.

You see people in ways that support your story of them. What would it look like if you changed your story? Nagging turns into a caring concern. The advice you took as criticism really was incredibly wise or helpful.

I missed out on having a friend for so many years. I missed out on a chance to be kind. I was cruel. I saw that my mom was struggling, and I ignored her. I am so grateful I can make things right with her and be friends with her now. That's why repentance and sin are so wonderful. I was a child. I didn't know any better. I couldn't have done anything differently based on what I was believing at the time. As an adult, I can see where I missed the mark and where I can do better. I've been given the gift to see my mom as she truly is, as God sees her.

I have forgiven my mom fully. When I think about her, I feel nothing but love for her. She has taught me very important lessons in my life. She was my biggest influence growing up and had the biggest impact on me - a great teacher. At the time I couldn't see that. I was so critical of her growing up. I expected her to be something for me and when she wasn't, I resented her and pushed her away. I didn't want to do that anymore.

All for Me

I started to question some thoughts that were stopping my ability to fully love my mother. One of these thoughts was, "Mom should never be late." This was a hard one to get passed. It's hard because the principle of being early to things so that you are prepared and not rushed is so much more attractive to me. If someone is relying on me, I don't want to keep them waiting either. My mother oftentimes was late picking me up from dance class. When class got out, all my friends would dash out and jump in their cars waiting for them outside the studio. I was eager as well to get home and relax after a long day of school and lessons. Sometimes I didn't have to wait long, but there were times where I was the last one to get picked up. I hated being the last one. When she finally arrived, I would impatiently push for answers: "What took so long? I was waiting forever!" I didn't really care about an excuse. In my mind, being late was wrong no matter the reason.

I knew that feeling this way about anyone did not feel good to me. It wasn't patient or forgiving. It was harsh, and I did not want to be that kind of person. With that in mind, I took that thought and was going to explore it and look to the opposite thought. The thought, "Mom should be late." came to mind. I sat there for a minute. It was hard to get past the feelings that it was wrong to keep people waiting. Nevertheless, I waited for something to come. I looked to see what my mom had been doing, or what she often did while I was in dance class. I saw her in my mind running errands. Again, I thought, "Why does she try to cram in all these errands

when she knows she only has a certain amount of time?" So, I waited for something else to come into my mind. I repeated again, "My mom should be late. Why?" Then I saw it. I saw the groceries in her car. Groceries that I would likely eat. After that realization, I started to realize something that changed my entire view. She should be late because she was busy running errands for me and for my family. It's not like she went to the movies or a manicure. She was working so that I would have everything I needed to be comfortable and taken care of.

When I saw this for the first time, I got very emotional, especially since I am now a mother and I am experiencing first hand all the things you sacrifice to be a mom and all the work that goes into it. It's truly a thankless job. She was doing all those errands for me! On the days she was late, she was trying to fit in just one more thing for me. Because I didn't see this gift she was providing, I jumped into the car and treated her very coldly. I showed ingratitude and entitlement. These are traits I do not wish to carry with me. At that moment, I saw where I had been wrong and how I had hurt her.

The last important finding I discovered was, "I should be on time (or early)." I see that without being focused on judging my mom on what's right or wrong, I discover the principle that I want to live. It's important to me to be early to things. As an adult I don't try to squeeze in extra things, or sign up for more than I can handle. It makes life easier for me and I feel more in control of my time. I practice proactive ways to be on time and learn what works best for me and what doesn't. I do not require anyone else to be that. I do it because I want to do it. However, when I looked again, I saw that, "I should never be late," was a lot of pressure to put on myself. I don't want to be late, but sometimes I will be. Can I be gentle with myself when I am late instead of panicked? Can I look ahead to next time and what I need to do to not feel rushed or be angry with little kids and their lack of urgency? I hope I can be that for myself.

In many ways, my mom lived for me. She gave me such a wonderful childhood. For one, she is an amazing gift giver. She always gave me the exact thing I wanted or the exact thing I never knew I wanted. Also, she was the best when it came to sick days. She would pick up a Seventeen Magazine, my favorite drinks, and I got to watch tv all day. She was kind and attentive. I loved being sick - except for the feeling like garbage part of sickness. She is also incredibly generous - the most generous person I know. She often works extra shifts and overtime just so she can give all her six kids, our spouses, and her grandchildren epic Easters and Christmases. She loves to travel. If you tell her a place you've been dreaming of going, she will dream up the whole trip and make it happen. I got to experience so many different things growing up. Mainly, she taught me what empathy was. She knows how to anticipate others' needs and is always respectful to the person she is speaking to. She calls everyone sir and ma'am. I can see countenances change when she does that. I could go on and on.

There are things my mom does that I do not wish to do myself. So I don't. There are things that I remember were very hurtful to me growing up. I wished she had been kinder or had kept a piece of advice to herself. I acknowledge that as a child there were times that I felt completely misjudged by her and my feelings hurt by her. When I go back to a childhood memory in my mind's eye, do I soak up and relive that same pain again and again? If I do, that pain is not from my mother - it is ONLY from me. The thing that happened, happened once. If you are inflicting that pain on yourself over and over again from a memory, you also have the power to end it. Acknowledge the hurt, question it, then forgive. But only if you want to be free.

Humanize Mothers

We are so hard on our mothers. Elizabeth Gilbert, author of Eat Pray Love, left this Mother's Day message on her Facebook page, "...We never stop blaming the mothers, do we? How many years, how many dollars, how much energy have we all spent as a culture, talking about how mothers have failed us? What we, as a culture, expect from our mothers is merely that they not be human. Mothers are meant to be some combination of Mother Mary, Mother Teresa, Superwoman, and Gaia. It's a merciless standard of perfection. Merciless! God help your mother, if she ever fell short. God help your mother, if she was exhausted & overwhelmed...So this is my question: Can we take a break today from judging the mothers, and show them mercy, instead?"

She goes on to say that this doesn't mean the things you may have been subjected to at the hands of your mother were okay. The pain is real and there are consequences to actions. However, are we able to see the pain our mothers were in? As adults can we be compassionate and show them mercy and forgiveness for something that happened long ago? Mothers judge themselves enough. I know I have hurt my kids feelings many times. My fear makes me do things that deflate my kids or hurt their spirits. I just pray they will forgive me and see past my shortcomings. I hope they see how hard I am trying to make them feel loved and not take out my frustrations on them. Balancing love and correction is hard enough. I want my kids to feel loved and accepted through correction, just as I want to feel loved and accepted.

Mom, I'm sorry for resenting you and not being forgiving. I held on to pain to prove to myself that what you did was wrong. If one of my children held on to a hurt caused by me, I would be heartbroken. I would pray every day for their forgiveness. I'm sure there were nights where you have knelt and prayed for this very thing. I'm truly sorry. Being a mother is hard work. Navigating a marriage is hard work. We all are doing our very best - and sometimes our very best is still not enough. That's when grace steps in and reminds me that when I live in the now, I am living in a state of forgiveness - <u>looking at you, Mom, like you're brand new.</u>

CHAPTER 9

"I Need You to Accept Me"

Marriage

Marriage has a way of bringing out the bottom feeders of belief. They are like those "fish," monsters that live only in the deepest and darkest parts of the ocean. They are the ones that have the ferocious fangs and lights dangling from the top of their heads. These thoughts can bring out really scary things. I don't know what it is about intimate relationships that trigger those deep underground beliefs, but it's only a matter of time before they surface and wreak havoc on your happiness.

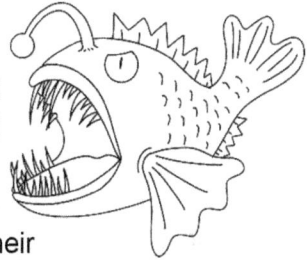

My marriage to Loren is very different from my first. Unlike Rick, I married Loren without any deep story coming in (as far as I knew). We also both did our due diligence to make sure all aspects of our unique lives were experienced, so that we knew we'd actually be a good fit. The relationships Loren had nurtured and cultivated with his ex needed to be preserved, and he needed to make sure I would be the best possible stepmom for Leah. I expected the same from him. We were very smart about everything, but it was the assurance of our love for each other that kept our fears away.

However, there were times when things did not go smoothly and Loren had the thought, "maybe it would be easier if I were single." When he'd share that with me the thought that came to me was, "I need Loren to adore me at all times." These bottom feeding fish-like fears, lurk for prey in the dark. They wait for their chance to bite in any circumstance that calls for it.

Criticism

It started off with small things. Loren would tell me what I should and shouldn't do when it came to cooking and cleaning. It was annoying. I didn't understand why it mattered to him so much. I felt like if he's not doing it, he shouldn't have a say. Just eat the chicken and be grateful, you know? I decided to question the thought, "Loren is critical." When you think of someone in critical condition medically, it means they are in crisis of a disease or injury. The greek word for crisis is krinein. Krinein means to decide or make a judgement. Roughly, it is the turning point of a disease when a decision must be made to save a life. The word disease is broken up to mean dis-ease, or a lack of ease. You could even call it inconvenience.[25] This time I decided to rewrite the thought based on my new found definitions, "Loren is deciding I have reached a point where the task I am doing, or the belief I have, is inconveniencing me or causing me more work." Therefore, Loren sees a struggle and wants to make things easier for me. He may even be saying to himself, "I want to make things easy for Emily so that she is happy." When I look at it this way, criticism sounds like a positive thing. Besides, I already could

---

[25] "Critical: Definition of Resist by Oxford Dictionary on Lexico.com Also Meaning of Resist." *Lexico Dictionaries | English*, Lexico Dictionaries, 2020, www.lexico.com/en/definition/critical.

see from the opposite thought that I was being critical of Loren for trying to help me.

Granted, I was still a little annoyed by his "help." I thought to myself, "Loren is so particular." I could not shake that feeling that I was being nitpicked. So, in the spirit of finding other meaning, I looked up the word 'particular.' Particular means concern for a small detail. Breaking this down even further, concern comes from the Latin word, 'cerner,' which means to sift or discern. The word detail in Latin, 'talea,' means to cut.[26] Based on this, if I were to rewrite my thought it would instead be, "Loren is discerning and sifting through in his mind what is not needed and what practices should be cut out or discontinued." Then it hit me. Nothing about this process of his is meant to be personal. It is actually just the way his mind ticks. So why do I take it so personally?

I clammed up whenever I felt him hovering over my shoulder watching me cook - "he's judging me, I know it." Why did I do that? If I didn't have the thought, I would just think he was admiring my handiwork, curious about my methods, or just wanting to know how soon he could eat! All these are so much better thoughts. Why does criticism feel so personal to me? Then I recognized a familiar feeling. It's the same feeling that came as a little girl getting in trouble by my mother. It's me sobbing on the carpet in my room because I didn't do what I was 'supposed' to do. It's the same feeling I get when I don't feel loved because I did something wrong in my loved one's eyes. It was a crippling feeling and it happened often in our marriage (and honestly it sometimes still does). I could finally

---

[26] "Particular: Definition of Resist by Oxford Dictionary on Lexico.com Also Meaning of Resist." *Lexico Dictionaries | English*, Lexico Dictionaries, 2020, www.lexico.com/en/definition/particular.

put words to the thought that was troubling me most: "I need you to accept me. I need your love."

Is it Love?

Back in April of 2017 Loren and I got into the biggest argument we have had since being married. I was very pregnant and very grumpy at the time. On our walk to school, Leah was being short towards Achilles and yelled at him to move, so I yelled at her, "Leah, how about you ask what Achilles is doing instead of yelling at him to move!" I also explained that Achilles waits at the top of the hill for me because he likes to race me down the cement sidewalk. Leah was obviously shaken by this. I felt bad for yelling, but didn't think my correction was in the wrong. Loren apparently did not like what he heard and skipped away on his boot with the help of his crutches (he was recovering from an injury to his Achilles tendon but still insisted on coming on our walks to school). I knew immediately that he was annoyed at me for having a bad attitude. I was annoyed with myself too! So, I took the walk home as an opportunity to hit the reset button and just chill the heck out.

I got home feeling the effects of my walk of solitude, ready to move on. Loren did not. He went quickly to his car in the driveway and straight to work. This was a Wednesday morning. He planned to leave that afternoon for a business trip to Dallas, and when he came home to pack he still wanted to be angry and not talk to me. He was very cold. It made me quite sad. I tried to approach him and ask him if he could help me with something. He said he was busy and to see if there was someone I could call...okay jerk. I was really upset now. It wasn't until the next day when I saw my texts weren't being delivered that I figured out Loren had blocked my phone number. That hurt my heart so badly. I felt rejected and unloved, and to top it all off, I was 35 weeks pregnant. I was unable to contact my husband if his baby were to come early or if something were to happen to me. It made me feel that he didn't even care at all about me.

I didn't hear a single peep from him Wednesday late afternoon until Saturday morning. I couldn't believe he had blocked me for 3 days! A friend I had confided in wanted to make it clear to me that his behavior was in fact abusive and neglectful. I agreed this was a hurtful pattern, a pattern of behavior he knew hurt me. Loren would often leave anytime we had a disagreement or if he was just annoyed with me. I hated when he would do this, because I am quite dependent on knowing that he still adores me. I figured I could suffer for about a day and call it "respecting his process," but that was my limit. He had promised he would never go more than a day without seeking reconciliation with me. He broke that promise to me, and my ego was screaming.

I was very anxious to talk to him to make him aware of this abusive behavior and prayed that he would see his wicked ways and wrongdoings, come to his senses and make a drastic change. It was that, or else I didn't think I could be in this relationship anymore. I was full of fear. The conversation was off to a rough start.

Loren did not like being accused of abuse or neglect and continued to be short and cold. I began to panic, like really panic, and aggressively sobbed, practically begging him to see my side. Loren was shaken up by my panic and tearful cries. He expressed to me that he didn't want me to be sad and apologized for breaking his word to me. I couldn't speak. I was too busy hyperventilating and trying to calm down. At this point, I was having a full-blown panic attack. My entire spirit felt as though it had melted into the floor. My body felt limp and darkness consumed me. At that moment I felt damned. I felt doomed to be in another abusive relationship with someone who didn't care if they hurt me or not. I got into the shower to try and continue to calm down, but couldn't. The sobs were nonstop.

When I got out of the shower, I tried again to beg for Loren to see how badly he was hurting me and stop this behavior of leaving me when he gets annoyed. Again, no luck. He was getting really frustrated at this point. The thing that took me over the edge was when Loren used this phrase, "You can either accept my process, or you can leave." That phrase was my kryptonite. It was my marriage to Rick. I was forced to either accept the things happening to me or leave. The beliefs of, "if you really loved me you wouldn't hurt me," and, "he would change this one thing for me if he really loved me" came up. His refusal to do so meant he didn't love me and he didn't care.

Whenever Loren leaves the house after an argument, the same thoughts I formed earlier in life awaken inside me. Those thoughts include, "I'm only worthy of love when I'm perfect," and "I'm only worthy of love when I'm being my best self," and I had plenty of memories from my past to pull from for evidence. Memories would flood in of my mom yelling at me as a child for not doing things her way or to her satisfaction. Also, memories of my family, especially my father, pushing me away after I got pregnant the first time, made me experience the same feelings of rejection all over again. I felt like I didn't deserve their love and acceptance in my imperfect state. Those thoughts popped into my mind the moment Loren walked away from me after dropping the kids off at school and continued to fester for 3 days straight.

I've been working on respecting Loren's process of needing time on his own after an argument since the first time he did it. I did not like it, but I put aside my beliefs that it was wrong of him to do so and saw instead that it was helpful for him. I tried to not take it personally. By leaving, he could press his own reset button and work out the negative thoughts he was having on his own. Besides, I had created that safety-net of the "one day of space" rule we had previously agreed on. I could survive one day. It was uncomfortable, but I managed. Past one day though, I felt pain, pain, pain. After the 3rd day, the pressure had built up to the point that my depression was spewing all over the place like a leak in a dam finally eroding the dam's walls, leading to its eventual breakdown and failure. Loren walking away symbolized everyone in my life that turned their face from me because of the choices I made. I believed in that moment that Loren did not love me. I told myself this because Loren stopped being affectionate, ceased giving me words of affirmation, and a clear look of disdain towards me had taken over his countenance. I would tell myself that I do not deserve his love when I am being grumpy. This belief and all the others swarming around my head caused me great suffering. In a nutshell, I was stuck between two bookends of thought. One being, "if he really loved me, he would see how much his actions hurt me and change," and "I'm only worthy of Loren's love when I am perfect." On the other hand, I believed I deserved to be loved, admired, and accepted at all times. I'm allowed to be upset with Loren, but he was not allowed to be upset with me. Is that love?

My ego/Satan was delivering a crystal-clear message to my subconscious. That message was, "don't let, or allow yourself, to be abused by another man again." This was my state of being. In that mindset, I was very afraid. Sitting on the edge of my bed, my damp towel wrapped around my pregnant belly, I prayed. I closed my eyes and I told God how scared I was and to just tell me what it would look like if I were to be submissive to Loren. I knew that submission was the opposite of what the Devil was proposing. The part of me that wanted to protect myself screamed at this request. "Being submissive to abuse is weak! Don't lose yourself again into depression!" I again asked God, "Please show me what it would look like if I were submissive to Loren and gave him what he was asking for. What would you do? Who would you be at this moment?" Immediately following my request, all of the stressful thoughts fell away. A soft thought arose in me that said,

> *"Put aside the fears of being abused and neglected, or ideas of worthiness of love, and come again with a clear mind and no story to listen to what Loren is asking for."*

I looked again to what Loren was asking for and this is what I found. Loren wants space, absolute freedom, and control of how he works out his annoyances. He doesn't want to be told when to reconcile. He wants to be able to communicate at a time he can give his full attention to me (not on a business trip for example).

While I was on the bed, I invited Loren over to me. He laid on his side facing me, ready to hear what I was going to say. He was obviously still frustrated, but lovingly showed his willingness to listen. I told him my prayer and about the haunting thoughts I was having. I told him what being submissive looks like, and that's what I would do for him from now on. (I actually meant it.) As soon as I spoke, all panic left me. I was calm and still. Loren had a tear leave his eye. He acknowledged how hard that must have been for me to say. His guard came down as well and instead of feeling like he was backed into a corner, I gave him the freedom to evaluate if this was the kind of husband he wanted to be.

When you look at a situation with fear as your scope, you cannot come to a peaceful conclusion. I either would have reluctantly said, "fine do whatever you want," and been depressed any time we had an argument, or left the marriage feeling terribly heartbroken having to leave my best friend for what I thought was for my protection. It would have been especially confusing because I know Loren wasn't and isn't an abusive person. Far from it!

Without the beliefs running the conversation, I was able to relinquish control over Loren, and my need to be right, and just listen to his side. Then, without an agenda, I was able to speak to Loren with the sole purpose of trying to better understand him. I asked him what made it so hard for him to be around me when I am being grumpy or upset? Specifically, I asked him, "Why is it that when Leah is grouchy or upset you try to make her smile and laugh, but you don't do that with me? You will even do that with complete strangers, but with me, you don't. You leave instead. Why is that?"

Loren took a minute to look why that was the case. He shared with me that whenever I am grumpy or upset, he takes it very personally, even when it is not geared toward him. When I am not being my pleasant, happy self, his instinct is to run away from me, and not be around my negativity. We were not as different as I thought. So, for whatever reason, when I'm not happy he takes it very personally and instead of wanting to make me happy, he chooses to leave instead. When I was being grumpy, even though it wasn't directed at him, he wanted an apology from me. Confused by this, I asked him why it affected him that way. He shared with me that he believed when I am being grumpy, I am not being loving. If I am not being loving, I can't possibly love him at that moment either.

Upon hearing that, I saw that he was right. I apologized to Loren for making him feel I didn't love him at that moment. It's true I didn't like him. I thought he sucked. The truth is I don't ever stop loving Loren, and he doesn't stop loving me. People that truly love each other, like the way we love each other, wouldn't intentionally hurt the other. In reality we are really just hurting ourselves by the thoughts we are believing about the other person. It's not that Loren stops loving me. He thinks I don't love him and his response is to leave. I could finally see that he did love me the whole time. It was my beliefs that told me he didn't.

The thought, "I'm only worthy of Loren's love when I am perfect," became irrelevant. The opposite was actually true. "I'm worthy of Loren's love when I am being imperfect." This was true because his love for me never stopped, even when I was being grumpy. It was his own beliefs that told him that, "When Emily is grumpy, she doesn't love me." <u>We both are the same</u> in that we both hope for unconditional love, but are blindsided by our own stressful thoughts that try to convince us that the other's love has gone away. After seeking to understand Loren, instead of changing him, I saw that it was his own belief about my grumpiness that was causing his wanting to be separate from me. His

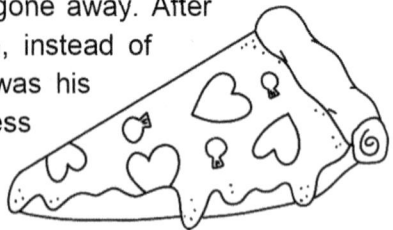

own story. When I was able to step out of my own fearful story, I could seek to understand him. His story had nothing to do with me, and his leaving had nothing to do with me, just as my grumpiness had nothing to do with him. After our conversation we felt more connected than ever before. Then we got some pizza. Pizza fixes everything.

The next time I saw Leah I apologized to her. I told her I should have been more kind and was sorry. She was also sorry for yelling at Achilles. We hugged and that was that. I also told her about hormones and if I seemed grumpy it had nothing to do with her. I was just being flooded with all kinds of things to help the baby grow and it can turn me into a monster sometimes. We laughed.

The higher-self is always unconditional love. When there is a story added to a situation, the ability of being loving or not being loving is governed by what the ego, natural man, or Devil convinces you into believing. The truth is, I love because I AM love. Everything else is just an added story, even if it is a nice story.

We Are The Same

What I realized as well was that Loren and I react the same way when we are feeling like the other person does not love us. We retreat. We fall out of love in that moment as our love is replaced with fear. When we are fearful, we seek to protect ourselves from harm - from a broken heart. I don't want to be around Loren either when he is not showing warmth and kindness. With that said, is that true love? Or is true love letting the other be angry because they are working through something that is really just only hurting themselves. Was Loren really hurting me? Was his anger meant to harm me, manipulate me, and change me? This is a very important question to ask because for some people the answer is yes. But, the truth is, you can never know for sure. That's why it's important to look at the opposite to see IF that could also be true.

When I looked at Loren, I knew that was not the kind of person he was. I knew what manipulation and narcissism looked like. I've even studied it academically. No, Loren was not that. Then I looked back at myself with that judgement turned around on me, "I am being manipulating. I am being narcissistic." I saw truth in those statements as well. I was trying to manipulate Loren into changing by showing him the level of sadness I could get to. I wanted him to see my panic attack. I was being narcissistic at that moment because all I cared about was for him to change to appease me. I only cared about my happiness at that moment. I wasn't trying to be those things at the time. I was just too blinded by sadness to realize my mistake. Does that make me a manipulator and a narcissist? No, but it gave me the chance to see where I was in the wrong. I gave myself the freedom to take a step back and evaluate if that is the person/wife I wanted to be.

What Are You Thinking?

While you were reading the story of our argument did you notice that voice in you forming an opinion of its own about the situation? Did it tell you Loren was out of line? Did it tell you I was overreacting? The ego is great at that. The gift of the Devil is not about seeing who's right and who's wrong and then trying to convince the other how in the wrong they are. That tactic will most likely fail. Dale Carnegie said, "A man convinced against his will is of the same opinion still." If a person feels they are forced into changing themselves, it will be met with reluctance and fear. I want freedom to choose for myself what I want to change and what I don't based on my values and personal principles. I'm sure Loren wants the same courtesy.

The gift of the Devil is also not about finding evidence to build up your case on all the ways you were right to make you feel justified in your plight. That tactic does not serve you or leave you with peace. <u>The gift of the Devil is about seeing how the need to be right has taken over your peace of mind, which in turn tells you that that is the exact belief that needs to be questioned.</u> There are still many stressful thoughts that come up when I feel like Loren is upset with me, because I feel such happiness whenever we are on good terms. Because of that, I work the atonement on each thought and try on the perspective of the opposite to see what truths I am missing. In doing so, I find a beautiful new truth every single time.

If we have an argument and Loren leaves emotionally, I notice that I sometimes leave him too. We are the same in that respect. I know that it sometimes takes leaving so that you can have time to work it through. The leaving is done in hopes that it will help us be closer. That is love to me. That is how I see it. Since then, Loren hasn't physically left for as long as he did. It's not because I convinced him not too, but because the meaning for me changed from fear of rejection into a process to reconcile. Without that fear and pressure on Loren and myself, there hasn't been a need to flee. Until it happens again that is, and if it does that's okay too. That's how I choose to see it and it has brought me peace knowing that I don't need Loren to accept me at all times. The opposite is actually true. I need me to accept Loren and his process because it will lead him back to me. I need to accept me and know that I'm going to mess things up and disappoint people from time to time. I am not defined by a past mess or mistake; I am defined by who I want to be in every moment. Besides, it is through disappointment and the mess that allow people to question their own stressful thoughts if they choose to. Why would I want to deny that freedom for them? That would not be love.

Seeking to Understand

There is a common cycle that Loren and I sometimes become trapped into. In one scenario, I may come to Loren and let him know what I am upset about. If Loren doesn't see my side, immediately agree with me, or say the phrase, "I can see how that upset you," I don't feel like he is trying to understand me. If instead he chooses to be defensive and tell me how I was wrong, I grow continually more agitated. I will continue to bring up the subject days later, and if I'm still not convinced that he is seeking to understand me, then we have real problems. Loren just wants me to let things go. I want him to understand me. I want to be heard. I want my feelings validated. When they are not, I feel betrayed and unloved, and tend to shut down.

As I work it out with God, praying that he will help me stop this cycle, I am inspired by this question that came to my mind: "Who are you to tell people how they should be? Making people be what you think you need from them is a fool's task." I could see that I was doing that. I was believing that if someone loves you, they will be what you need them to be for you. This was definitely the cause of my pain. I then felt inspired to look at the opposite thought, "If they love you, they will be themselves." That belief brought me peace. I knew that the truth of it was that seeking for Loren's understanding was just the front I was using to get my way. I had evidence of the principle being a powerful tool in relationships. Stephen Covey, one of Loren's favorite mentors, preaches this same principle. So, I knew my desire to be understood and accepted was good and right. The truth was I wanted Loren to be different for me. I wanted him to change. I wanted him to see how I was frustrated. I also wanted him to express to me that he wouldn't do it again. In other words, I was right and he was wrong. Loren is much too smart; he could see through that agenda as clear as water. Because he knew what I wanted, he would not give it to me. It was a twisted game of manipulation between us. Beyond that initial desperation to be understood by him, the opposite showed me something else. Who really was needing to be understood? It was ME. I needed to understand myself. I needed to understand this about me: I don't feel safe to be in a state of upset because of my fear that Loren will leave me if I'm not positive and perfect all the time. In other words, I wanted permission to be authentic without consequences.

<u>My deepest desire was to understand myself and to be able to express myself without fear.</u> I wanted to understand what belief was behind my upset, a belief that would continue to hold my peace hostage if I did not look at the source. I am powerful when I seek to understand myself. When that is the focus, I become more accepting of myself. I feel safe to feel upset, even knowing that in the past it has upset Loren. I know that it is not about Loren, it is about me. I accept myself as I am being in the moment, even if it isn't kind or warm. When I have the time to work it out in my head, and Loren is offended, he has every right to be - just like I do. Who am I to tell him how to be? I want him to be himself and feel safe being himself, just as I would want. I am genuinely sorry when I am

being rude and cold to Loren, because I know that hurts. It hurts me when it happens to me.

Sometimes the principle "seek first to understand then to be understood," can become a distraction. Because you know this is a good principle and a good way to be, you may expect the other person to practice the art of seeking to understand as well. If you feel like they aren't, things can get a little dicey. We tell ourselves we just want to be understood. We want the other to see our side. We seek validation. We hope that we can change their mind, or really just change the way we think they see us. When they don't, the war wages on. Why does it have to be a war - me against you? Seek to be understood - a phrase misunderstood. Understanding is not defending. It is not fighting for what's right or wrong. That's the distraction. Instead, try saying, "This is how I see it." When the other person shares, respond with two simple words, "Thank you." Peace prevails when the goal is not "I need to be understood," but instead is, "How can I help?" Try seeing that your partner is upset and unsettled. Try seeing that you are not the cause, only that your loved one is suffering. "How can I help? What can I do?" As long as personal values are honored, I'll do anything for the ones I love. I seek to understand what they are asking for. I can even help them piece it together - they may not know themselves. Then it becomes a request from my husband to me. That's what lovers do.

I Need Loren's Love?

I know that unconditionally loving Loren means honoring his process, because that's what I would want. It means showing him kindness and warmth after I've apologized, even if his feelings are still hurt and he wants more time to be distant. It's not demanding him to change for my comfort. It also means allowing myself to feel sad and hurt if that's how I'm feeling. It means seeking to understand myself so that I can be free of the pain I am ultimately causing myself. If I know this but still believe I need Loren to accept and love me at all times, I will continue to struggle in our relationship.

When I am not seeing with eyes of "I need Loren's love and acceptance," I know that what I really need is for me to love and accept myself. Here's what that looks like for me. For one, I am free to establish my own process for overcoming personal struggles. I can tell Loren what happened to cause an upset within me and apologize for being cold and resentful towards him. That's what I would want. Also, I'm not asking him to change, and I'm not asking him to admit fault. I'm taking 100% responsibility for myself. That's all I can ever do. As wise Maya Angelou has said, "Now that I know better, I can do better." Taking responsibility is a more powerful place to be because I control the outcome. In all, I don't need Loren's love to be happy. To be truly happy, I need to love myself and know I am responsible for my own happiness.

One more statement that came from, "I need me to love and accept Loren," was the opposite, "I don't need to love and accept Loren." For a moment it felt like I shouldn't think that way. It's not kind! However, something came to me when I entertained the thought. The phrasing, "I NEED to love and accept Loren" felt forced. It felt like there's a pressure to be in love all the time. That pressure can't possibly be kind. It takes away the choice to love. Therefore, I changed the statement to, "I choose to love and accept Loren. I choose to be attracted to him and see all the things I find attractive in me." That felt the truest, the most kind. I'm attracted to him/in love with him until I'm not (and vice versa). When Loren and I are in an argument, or not seeing eye to eye, he becomes like an enemy. I don't want to be around him and he doesn't want to be around me. At that moment, neither of us are attracted to the other. In order to make the choice to come back to loving each other, we must do the work. I choose to love Loren when I want to only see him as 100% loveable. If I see him any other way, I'm not being who I want to be. The reason Loren and I are still together is because of this principle. It is what our relationship is founded upon. When we are growing and evolving for the better together, questioning our own thoughts that are causing us pain, we are choosing to be in love. I'm not claiming to be an expert in marriage, nor do I claim to be an expert on love. I can, on the other hand, be an expert learner in loving Loren.

Focus

Whenever I believe that I need love, or I need to be loved in a certain way, it's because my focus is on me. At a young age, I dreamed about a future husband and what he would be like. I thought about romance and how he would make me feel. I've come to realize now that I personally feel the most love when my focus is on others. If my focus is on what I think I need to feel loved, I'm going to be let down often. In that mindset, my happiness and self-esteem revolves around what my partner thinks of me or how they treat me. If I'm looking at my relationship that way, I often feel victimized or hurt if an interaction is not a positive one. When I don't take a negative interaction about me personally, I can then see that the person I am with is simply struggling. That way, I make it all about them: "The way they see me is really upsetting them." They may be really loud or angry about their struggles. That's okay. In all, when I am making another person's upset all about me,

I am personally hurt by it. On the other hand, when I see that the upset is how the other person sees me at that moment, I don't have to wallow. I can help instead - whatever that help needs to be. The "help" could even mean taking myself out of a dangerous situation and I can make that decision with clear eyes.

When your relationship is built around how you make each other feel, it's hard to maintain in my experience. When your relationship is built around values and working together to achieve a bigger goal, the connection becomes what you can accomplish together instead of having someone that exists to make you feel valued and worthwhile. I feel most loved when Loren and I are working towards our joint goal of leaving an impact on the world bigger than ourselves. Loren has even said he's more attracted to me when he sees me being generous and loving because he knows I'm being who I want to be. That's the most attractive.

You think after such a discovery I would be cured of ever being upset again in our relationship. Not so. It still hurts when Loren is angry with me. I still feel like when I was a child - disappointing the most important people I love. Their disapproving looks still haunt me today. I feel like my reaction to seeing my loved ones triggered by me has been coded into the reptilian part of my brain along with breathing. However, the good news is that I know the truth. If I fall back into that pain, I have done the work and can do the work again to help me remember the truth. I remember that I need to love myself, trust in the process, and look at my focus. If my focus is seeking for love, I will have a hard time finding it. I remember that to give love is to receive love, that's when I'm at my happiest. When I am in that state again, I can choose happiness and peace.

Arguments may not seem like the most enjoyable of processes in the moment, but Loren and I have come to respect them. An argument means an opportunity to become closer. Arguments are further and farther between now, as all those stressful beliefs are proven false one by one.

I Am Responsible for My Own Happiness

When your happiness is based on the state of the world around you or around how the people in your life see you, you will never be happy. No amount of people pleasing will save your status. One way or another you will fail them and they will be disappointed. When this is your state of being, your happiness is contingent on everything but you. I have experienced this many times. It is disheartening and isolating. Ironically, when I am living to please others, or to please Loren, it's not because I love them. It's really for selfish reasons. It is for the purpose of self-preservation. I'm innocent when I am in this mindset because it is coming from a belief learned in childhood. When I was being yelled at by my parents, I believed I was not worthy of love. When I was being praised, I must have done something good and so I was deserving of love. As an adult, I may logically know that seeking to please others will not bring me happiness; however, the foundation of my world was based on this belief and so was my self-esteem.

On the other hand, I realize that my impact is much greater when I know that I'm not here for me. I am actually here for others. God sent his son not to condemn the world; but that the world through Him might be saved.[27] God sent His daughter (me) not to condemn (inflict loss on), but that through

---

[27] John 3:17

her she might alleviate the loss and add joy to others. How am I to achieve such a feat if my focus is turned inward? When I am trying to please my friends and please my family by trying to be something I think they want me to be, I am not helping them. I am most certainly not helping myself.

When I am at my happiest, I never believe that something should or shouldn't be different than what it is. I practice the Golden Rule, always treating others the way I would want to be treated. I take the time to be quiet and reflect when I am upset instead of pouting or spewing negativity. I know that I just need time to understand myself. I affirm in myself how great and lovely I am as is. I don't rely on Loren or anyone else's praise. If I want something done, I put my head down and get the job done because I promised myself I would. I do what I need to do. I don't expect others to do things for me. I do things myself because I love myself. I take action instead of wishing for things to change. When I am not enough, because sometimes my best is simply not enough, I know that I can always improve. To convince myself that I am enough is distracting me from growth. Your identity is not measured on enough and not enough. A serving of icecream is based on that measurement. I am not food and you are not food. We can grow; we can develop; and we can become better. This is what I have created for myself in my life so that I am being Happiness. In this way of being, I am love, patience, kindness, and peace. That is happiness to me. When I fall out of that state of being it is because I am believing a stressful thought or am turning back to an old perspective. If that is the case, I know that there is something else there for me to learn. There is something else to discover about myself that my higher-self desperately wants me to be free of. The gift of the Devil shows me the way.

Choosing Loren

The gift of the Devil is my greatest tool in relationships. Satan will show you every flaw and every shortcoming in your partner. How wonderful! It reminds us that there's an opposite, and that peace in relationships comes from focusing on our partner's strengths. Get to know them! Loren and I have taken many personality tests on date nights. Many of them are incredibly insightful. When we focus on our strengths we are more creative and more understanding of the other. Problem solving is less personal and more solution focused. It has changed the way we speak and interact with each other, and it has allowed us to honor each other's unique perspective - not seek to change it.

Sometimes I wonder if being in a relationship is really worth all this struggle? It would be nice to not have to live with the comments and the opinions of another person. When Loren comments on a messy floor I often think, "just leave me alone." Or, "you have no idea how hard taking care of 3 under 3 is!" But what I fail to remember in that moment is that I'm sharing a life with someone. That is Loren's floor too. It's our shared responsibility and it's important to him to keep it clean. He is opening the conversation up to see who can get the floor clean. Do I have time? Does Loren have time? When the floor becomes a metaphor for my self-worth and wanting to be left alone and not giving a report as to why the floor isn't clean, I am being selfish. I am not thinking of him. If his comment ignites anything negative inside of me it is because I am believing something that is untrue. It's not criticism; it's a question. It's not a put-down; it's a question. It's not years of female oppression; it's a question. How can we get the floor cleaned up?

<u>Asking for a life with no struggle is asking for a life without growth.</u> Perfection is growth. It is not the absence of pain because you've figured something out. The struggle always exists. But that's where the greatest love you have ever known lives. It lives at the end of the struggle. That's why I choose Loren. That's why I have chosen to be married to him. Growth is love. Love comes through pain and sometimes through loss.

CHAPTER 10

"I Lose Everything I love"

Loss

From the age of 3 to 8, I lived in the beautiful southern town of Albany, Georgia. I loved it there. I loved the giant trees towering overhead. Their foliage acted as rows of umbrellas blocking out the hot sun while I played. I loved running through the tall grass and watching the colorful birds gossiping back and forth. Most of all, I loved my friends. I loved them fiercely. At that time, my friends were my whole life. When my dad lost his job at the city's newspaper my parents decided to take the family to Arizona for a fresh start. I was devastated. The thought of leaving the town I loved and the friendships I'd built shattered my world. My 8 year-old self thought I'd never recover.

When we arrived at our rental home in Mesa, Arizona I scowled in consternation as I scanned my new landscape. Right away I noticed that instead of grass, tiny rocks covered the ground. Instead of lush, green trees with thick trunks there were small, spiky trees with thin trunks. Also, I had never seen a cactus before. I thought they were interesting enough that I wanted to bring one home to study. I did this so many times before with pinecones and leaves that I didn't see a problem collecting one. I went inside the house and tore off a piece of paper towel and returned to the cactus. With great precision I carefully plucked off a piece of cactus, wrapped it in the paper towel, and rested it slowly on my open hand. I figured that if I was careful enough, I could avoid getting poked. I dashed back inside with my outstretched hand to show my mom what I had found. Without realizing it, the spines of the cactus had pierced through the paper towel and into my exposed palm. It was stuck. My mom was able to push the body of the cactus off my hand onto the ground with a stick, but tiny, almost microscopic, spines remained. She helped me extract them with tweezers. I was not happy. I believed this harsh landscape had betrayed me. Not only that, but it was ugly. It was brown, dull, and sharp. I didn't like it at all. Not only did I lose my friends, I lost my beautiful backyard.

Naturally, it wasn't long before I discovered new friends to play with. Since we moved into a great family neighborhood, I spent a lot of time riding my bike from one friend's house to another. I never forgot my friend's in Georgia, but the new friendships I developed became just as special.

As the years went on, I finally could see the beauty in the desert that I was fighting so hard to ignore. The mountains that surrounded us, the pink and purple sunsets, and even the cacti and desert flowers became beautiful to me. I found peace and joy in my new home. However, as I grew older, things at home became prickly and fighting became commonplace between my parents.

When I was 17, my parents finally divorced. From then on, it felt like my family was never the same. All my siblings were affected one way or another. My beliefs about families being together crumbled. I didn't think we would ever be together like we were again. In my heart, it felt like a huge loss.

Losing my family made me search for connections outside of it. That's when I met Rick. Later when I ended up losing our baby, I struggled with understanding why it happened. Why did I have to go through the embarrassment of telling my family just to end up losing the baby in the end? Not only that, but I wrestled in my mind with God to determine if the baby I lost to miscarriage was even considered alive. Did the soul of that baby ever meet its body? I wondered if I would ever get the opportunity to raise the baby that I felt was lost to me. Later when Rick and my relationship ultimately ended in divorce, I felt that loss again when dealing with child custody arrangements for Achilles (just 1 year-old at the time). I thought, in a way, I was losing my child and I didn't want to share him. As described in earlier chapters, in many ways I have been freed from these anxieties. However, one lingering thought remained around these traumatic events that I hadn't yet discovered.

Things Don't Belong to Me

On a recent family vacation, I woke in the early morning, before the sun, feeling uneasy. I couldn't stop obsessing over the fear of losing another potential life growing inside me. I was pregnant again with baby number four and fears about the possibility of losing this child resurfaced. I experienced similar stressful feelings when I was pregnant with Woody, but I buried them. This morning, however, I desired to take a look at why this fear haunted me so. As I pondered the idea of loss, I realized that these feelings were similar to feelings that I had leaving Georgia and my friends at 8 years old. I started to follow the breadcrumbs. I sat quietly and looked back at my life to see if I could find even more evidence of these feelings resurfacing. I didn't quite know what the main belief was that was causing me pain and uneasiness yet, but I followed the feeling to see where else it would take me. I waited to see what other memories came forward.

Growing up, I often had strong reactions over any personal item that was lost or ruined. I remember losing a cuff earring that I loved. I knew it was somewhere in my room, but I couldn't track it down. I had two friends over at the time, and when I realized I had misplaced it I went berserk. I started tearing every sheet and pillow off my bed while crying, "This is why I can't have nice things!" I coined that before Taylor Swift wrote the song! Looking back, I could see the stunned looks on my friends' faces. They froze, not quite sure what to do with the manic display they were seeing play out. My friend, Tara, softly stated, "We'll help you look for it," attempting to defuse the pressure in the room. We never found it.

A thought I had coupled with this memory was, "that's the reason I rarely buy nice things for myself." I had a fear they would be lost or ruined by me or another person. Also, in my experience of living with younger sisters it was a common belief that they were entitled to everything in my closet. I remember one morning I saw that my sister had taken a pair of stilettos and worn them to a party. The front of them were scuffed beyond repair and the stem was scraped and covered in mud and grass. I was so furious that I went into her room while she was sleeping and threw them at her peaceful sleeping head as hard as I could. She woke up with a loud, "OW!!" while I slammed her door behind me. I was curious why these memories came up when contemplating the fear of loss. I questioned why I had such a strong reaction associated with things that belonged to me. Then, softly, the reason entered my mind.

I saw that I was living in fear of having things I love taken from me. Losing my friends, losing my first baby, losing my virginity in a way I didn't plan for, losing my son to divorce, and losing other things I cared for made me afraid of it ever happening again. Therefore, I only loved enough to know I would be okay If I were to lose that thing. I would show love, but in an indifferent, unattached way. I lived to avoid the pain of loss and being hurt again, instead of passionately loving everything in my life. It was apparent in my parenting, my marriage, and my friendships. It's like one foot was in the door and the other was right outside it. I was not "all in" in any aspect of my life. My misscarriage was a strong reason for this.

The Inspirer

"Is there anyone here with you?" my doctor pressed. "No, it's just me," I answered with trepidation. I had been escorted earlier into a private office to wait for what I knew could only be bad news. "There was no heartbeat," he said unadorned. "We believe the baby passed within the last week." I immediately began to sob. I responded, "Are you sure?" It was the worst possible news I had ever received. Being a young mother at 18 was not my original plan, but I had decided to keep the baby and raise it. I even told my family, which was not pleasant. Regardless, I was ready to love that baby and give it everything I had. I couldn't possibly foresee that I'd end up losing the baby after all. The doctor seemed surprised at my reaction. He said on an exhale, "You mean you wanted it?" I was confused by his question. I answered through tears, "I don't know." Everything after was a blur. I got up, left his office, and drove home to await the inevitable.

(WARNING: This next paragraph describes my miscarriage in some detail and may be sensitive to some readers.)

That night I woke up abruptly from some intense cramping. I went to the bathroom and discovered blood. I did not know exactly what a miscarriage entailed, but I naively assumed that it would be like a period. I didn't think about having to pass a baby. I guess I missed that part in the doctor's office. Honestly, I don't think I was even told what to expect. I got in my car and went to the convenience store next door to get some sanitary pads and quickly returned home. The cramping continued to get worse. Suddenly, as I was sitting on the toilet, I felt a gush of water. I was shocked and realized that must have been my water breaking. That's when it hit me that I was about to give birth to an actual baby. Very soon after, I felt the baby's head move through me and it's lifeless body fell into the basin below. I stood up and turned around to look at it. Its head seemed largely disproportionate to its tiny body, but it looked like a real baby. I didn't know what to do. I stared down and asked myself, "Do I take it out? Should I wrap it in something?" It was late at night. My father was asleep in his room. I was alone. Standing there in the deafening silence I realized I was too afraid to touch it. I slowly reached for the lever and pulled it softly down. I flushed my baby away. Then, in a zombie like state, I cleaned myself up and went back to bed.

Miscarriages are personal and difficult. The reason I shared my experience here is because I regretted the outcome of the miscarriage. I wasn't upset at myself, because I knew I went through something I wasn't prepared for. But in hindsight, I wished I had done things differently. For years I thought about it from time to time, but brushed it away. I felt like it was in the past and nothing could be done.

More than 10 years later I started thinking about that day and didn't push it out of my mind like I had before. I wondered if there was anything I could do to rectify that night I had come to regret. I couldn't change the past, but could I make it right in my mind? I looked back to that night to see what I wished I had done differently. For one, even though I didn't know the gender, I wished I had named the baby. So, I searched for names. I pondered on what losing this baby meant to me. The event changed my life forever. It's the reason I decided to get pregnant again a year later. It's the reason for every important discovery I have ever made about myself. It's the reason I'm where I am today. Therefore, I chose a name that meant, "The Inspirer." Only myself, my husband, and older children know this name. It is sacred to us and I save it for us. The second thing I wished I had done differently was pick the baby up and take it somewhere beautiful to be buried.

On a beautiful and clear Sunday afternoon my family and I drove to my favorite spot near the Salt River. In this spot, towering red canyons line the river. The wild Salt River horses often come to enjoy the shade of the canyons and drink from the cool water. I took a stone that I had found in the desert and wrote the baby's name on it. Dressed in our Sunday best, my husband and two oldest kids took a short walk to the riverside. I dug a small, but deep hole, and placed the rock inside. After filling the hole, I proceeded to recreate the event that happened over 10 years ago in my mind.

With my family by my side, I spoke this soliloquy. "Baby, when you died, I picked you up, cleaned you, and wrapped you in my arms. I took you here to this beautiful place to be laid to rest. I gave you a name, 'The Inspirer.' Inspire means to breathe life into. That's what you did to me. You gave me new life. You are the reason for everything that I have now and I am forever grateful. I love you."

It was such a powerful moment for me. I made it right. Now the only thing left in my heart was love instead of regret.

Story of the Stone

"A wise woman who was travelling in the mountains found a precious stone in a stream. The next day she met another traveler who was hungry, and the wise woman opened her bag to share her food. The hungry traveler saw the precious stone and asked the woman to give it to him. She did so without hesitation. The traveler left, rejoicing in his good fortune. He knew the stone was worth enough to give him security for a lifetime. But, a few days later, he came back to return the stone to the wise woman. 'I've been thinking,' he said. 'I know how valuable this stone is, but I give it back in the hope that you can give me something even more precious. Give me what you have within you that enabled you to give me this stone.'" - Author unknown

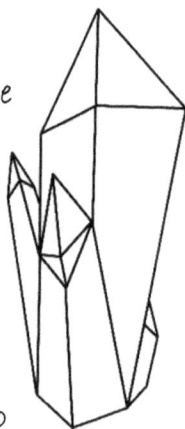

The story the Devil had delivered to me was that something most precious was taken from me. I was told that the pain I felt was because I had lost something I really loved and wanted - my first baby. It's the same story I've always had when it came to loss. I was also haunted by the thought that I would never know for sure if the baby was even considered alive. I believed these stories for a long time.

When the time was right for me, I decided to look at the opposite of this thought. The opposite thought for me was, "I gave away something most precious to me. Nothing belongs to me." That phrase sent an invigorating chill down my spine. That baby I thought I lost was not mine. It felt like a lie to say it was. Who am I to own another life? Next I wondered how I could give it away? What was "it"? The answer was, I gave away the thought the Devil had given me and replaced it with another. After giving away this thought, I was given another - one that came from God. That's how my baby made its way back to me. It made its way back in the form of a stone. It had come back, but this time with feelings of gratitude, love, and acceptance.

When my perspective was not on possession, the baby simply came and went like a beautiful dream. The pain I felt was not because of loss (even though at the time it was). The pain I felt was love. Nothing can be taken from me, because it is forever kept and pondered in my heart. Nothing in life is ever lost, but all is constantly shared and kept at the same time in a never- ending circle. I share the story of my personal stone as a gift to the world. I give it away freely and happily if anyone were to ask for it.

"The Inspirer" baby impacted the rest of my life. It took me down a path that led me right here, to this computer, writing this very sentence. It impacted me to show love to others and honor their process and their path. I am very sensitive towards my neighbor and hope to never offend, only uplift, even if I offend anyway. That baby's short life has not been short for me at all. It has been with me for over 10 years now, and it will always be with me. No matter when the soul meets the body, that baby lived to me. I am me, because of its life. Its physical 11 or 12 weeks with me turned out to be the greatest thing that could have ever happened to me. Its natural death allowed me the space to discover my relationship to God and why I even matter.

Denver Moore from the film "Same Kind of Different as Me" put into his own words this common idea, "The only thing that we keep forever is the thing that we give away." How do we keep that which we give away? There is a difference in thinking that something is taken from you vs. you giving something away. The first is a victim mentality. The latter is a gift that you freely give. A gift of love that you give leaves a lasting impact on the world for good. It is remembered warmly and will always be with you. The choice on how you see it is entirely yours.

I am young and know that the longer I live, the more I will experience death around me. I have seen the pain that comes from losing loved ones in unexpected or even horrific ways, so I do not wish to make light of loss. I recently listened to a mother speak about the worst day of her life. She had lost her husband and some of her children unexpectedly. I never was able to learn her name, but when she was speaking she said something that has stayed with me. She said, "I didn't want to go through the pain to know *Christ*." That made it clear for me the sacredness that is loss. It's painful to face the beliefs around loss and be willing to see the other hand - but, it is the only way to freedom and peace. ~~The opposite of joy is not sorrow; it is 'lack of knowledge.~~' Therefore, one can feel intense sorrow and at the same time feel joy in Christ, or in atonement. You feel joy knowing that the sorrow you feel is not from resisting or fighting what has happened. It is sorrow from loving another person.

Russell M Nelson, President of the Church of Jesus Christ of Latter-Day Saints said, "Mourning is one of the deepest expressions of pure love. It is a natural response in complete accord with divine commandment: 'Thou shalt live together in love, insomuch that thou shalt weep for the loss of them that die.'[28] Moreover, we can't fully appreciate joyful reunions later without tearful separations now. The only way to take sorrow out of death is to take love out of life."[29] It is a miracle to have and experience that level of love. It's in your heart forever and can never be lost or taken from you.

Forever With You

On December 6th, about 9 months after my miscarriage, Carrie welcomed her first daughter into the world. That beautiful little girl was held by her father, Loren Smith, for the first time in a hospital room somewhere in Mesa, Az. If my baby had survived to full term, it would have been delivered around that same time. After the belief I had surrounding loss was released from my mind, I was able to see that I had really lost nothing. I had Leah. I couldn't have known then that in only 5 years time I would become a second mother to that little girl. When I married Loren she became my eldest daughter. Leah

---

[28] The Doctrine and Covenants 42:45
[29] Nelson, Russell M. "Doors of Death." *The Church of Jesus Christ of Latter-Day Saints*, Apr. 1992, www.churchofjesuschrist.org/study/general-conference/1992/04/doors-of-death?lang=eng.

is 8 months older than Achilles. People think they are biological brother and sister. Even though it isn't physically possible, I like to think that she always was. I just had to wait until it was my time to join her family. I love that story I have of her. I feel it was a realization given by God to help me see what I was missing. I'm grateful that things can never be lost to me.

My Son

On a quiet walk one day in 2016, I started to name the things I saw - sky, tree, flower, rock, etc. Then I thought about my then 7 year-old son, Achilles. I said to myself, "my son." Then as an instinct I said, "my sky, my tree, my flower." It felt so bizarre for me to be claiming ownership of these things. Because I give something a name does not mean it belongs to me. Achilles, my son, does not belong to me. I may have created his physical body with a little help, but he is his own person. I made the choice to take care of him. I love him.

The sorrow that came was because I thought I was losing Achilles because I had to share him. Nevertheless, knowing the truth - that Achilles never belonged to me in the first place - I know I am unable to lose him. I share in the caring of him, as he cares for others too. If I do feel sorrow, I know it's because I love him so much and want him to grow into his true and greatest potential. That is the truth.

<u>Negative thoughts do not belong to me either. They only become mine if I take them on as my identity.</u> Thoughts come, and they go. I choose which ones to believe and which ones I don't. I am the creator of my reality and I create the person I want to be. Before I could do this, there was one more thought I needed to overcome.

CHAPTER 11

"I Can Never Get it Right"

Expectations

With how vast social media has become, at our fingertips are the stories of real people and their real, everyday struggles. I see more and more the admittance of women, especially mothers, feeling like they aren't good enough or are falling short. I think the honesty and realness is fantastic. It takes courage to share personal things that aren't picture perfect. When I read those "I'm not enough" posts, I remember times when I had similar feelings about my own mothering and self-worth. My personal belief was, "I can never get it right." By using the Devil's gift to find the truth, I can honestly say I do not believe those thoughts any more. I have become so practiced in the art of questioning my thoughts, that they aren't allowed to dwell in my head anymore. They may come, but they don't affect me, because I simply don't believe them. That doesn't mean I don't recognize when I know I wasn't doing my best. It just means there is no self-judgement. If I knew how to be different in that moment, I would have been different. But, I only know what I know in the moment.

During that time of truth finding I wanted to understand what the phrase "being enough" even meant. What is "enough?" What was I comparing myself to to measure whether I was enough or not? Enough for what? Enough for whom? I then thought of the word expectation. I felt that expectations are strongly linked to feelings of being enough or not. If certain expectations you have put on yourself are not met, there are likely feelings of inadequacy and failure to follow.

The word expectation comes from the Latin word *exspectare* meaning "to look out for." The Latin word *expect* also means to "defer action," or "to wait." Expectation therefore means, "watching and waiting."[30] In other words, it means figuratively sitting around judging others and ourselves. When we are in a state of judging others and judging ourselves, we are too busy to take personal action towards being who we want to be. We are comparing ourselves instead of simply being who we want to be and doing what we want to do. Have you ever compared yourself to another person? I watched a news story of a mother being arrested for leaving her child locked in a basement while she got high on Meth. I thought to myself, "I'd never do that" and "At least I'm not that bad." I had also seen mothers on Instagram post pictures of extravagant themed birthday parties where everything was handmade. I would think, "I suck at throwing fun parties for my kids" and "They are so much more creative than me." A spectrum was created in my mind. Super Instagram Mom was at the top and Meth Mom was at the bottom. My worth and happiness was determined on where I put myself on this spectrum.

Expectations paralyze personal progress. That's why I no longer believe, "I am not enough." I realized that the concept

---

[30] "Expectation: Definition of Lucifer by Oxford Dictionary on Lexico.com Also Meaning of Lucifer." *Lexico Dictionaries | English*, Lexico Dictionaries, 2020, www.lexico.com/en/definition/expectation.

"enough" only existed if I was watching, waiting, and comparing myself to others. Without expectations and comparisons there can finally be space for action - for creativity and discovering what your truest desires are. This is accomplished by minding your own business and asking yourself, "What kind of person do I want to be?" If you are not being the person you want to be, you can look to see how you can course-correct. Then instead of comparing yourself to others, you find other people that are great examples of your values and use them as mentors and motivators. Of course, sometimes our best is not enough to accomplish what needs to be done. Sometimes we will fail. Sometimes instead of being our best selves, another person takes control. I like to call her Scary Mommy.

Scary Mommy

I have this person inside me; I refer to her as Scary Mommy. Scary Mommy is a raging beast woman. She is rude, mean, and out of control. Forget counting to 10, once Scary Mommy is out, it takes a good night's sleep or walking away to silence her. SM came out once while I was trying to get the house cleaned and my family packed up to leave on a trip to Mexico. I did not have a whole lot of time, seeing that it was a last-minute decision to go. I enrolled my kids to help me clean (they were 8 at the time) and gave them specific tasks. I enrolled them in the possibility that if they helped, we could spend a whole extra day at the beach. At that age, if there was ever the feeling of "rush" or "haste" in the air, my Achilles could not emotionally handle himself. He would break down in tears and do his best to go as s. l. o. w. as p. o. s. s. i. b. l. e. My daughter will put her head down and get to work. She probably feared SM and learned early on what would trigger Her release and how to avoid it. SM was full-fledged out by the middle of the day. I was stomping around as though I was wearing combat boots and carrying a rifle. I went from room to room, very focused and working as quickly as possible. Achilles was following me around with puppy dog eyes and crocodile tears, telling me he had hit his head (again).

SM told him she didn't care. He tried to hug her. SM said, "I don't want your hugs."

Achilles said, "I don't like being rushed, Mom."

SM crassly answered, "Well I don't like hearing you whine. I refuse to raise lazy, ungrateful children." (YIKES)

Oh, she was terrible! By the end of the day, we weren't able to finish everything in time to leave to make the border, so we ended up not going early at all. I was extremely disappointed that night. I tried so hard to prepare to leave early so that everyone could have that extra day at the beach, but OH MY, the cost! The cost was my children's and my husband's happiness. SM destroyed their sweet spirits. Before going to bed that night, I told my husband how awful I was being and listed out loud all the terrible things SM said and did. I felt terrible. I especially felt awful for saying those things to Achilles. Even though I knew what I had done was wrong, I did not fall into the trap of kicking myself over and over. Those thoughts of inadequacy still NEVER entered my stream of thought. Why? Because I already determined long ago that I am always a good enough mom. I may have not been enough, but I am enough. I may have failed, but I am no failure. In every single moment, I am enough because I was being all I knew how to be. Even when I was being SM. SM gives me the opportunity to use the gift of the Devil. It puts me face to face with the person I don't want to be and allows me to pick up important truths that I may not be aware of.

Knowing that being rushed brings SM out, I asked myself if it was worth the cost of my family's happiness? If I had succeeded in having everything ready, would an extra day at the beach have evened out the crazy? Honestly, no. The damage had been done. With this realization I decided that the next time I would simply say, "Based on the time allotted and the time it takes to carry out an early exit, it's a no for me." Or "I've got my list, I'm going to do my best, if you guys want to contribute and help move this process along then we may have a shot. If not, then chances are it's a no." I found that the true Emily doesn't mind the eustress (the good stress) of rushing and meeting a goal. I actually perform quite well when there's a countdown. It helps me focus. It's the beliefs surrounding being rushed that bring out SM. Beliefs like, "My kids need to work faster." "No one cares that I'm working so hard for them." "If I don't push Achilles now when he's young to work as quickly and as effectively as me, he'll grow up to be a lazy worker who doesn't jump at the opportunity to help." "My kids are ungrateful if they do not do chores and contribute." "Why do I even bother making the kids help? They only make the process much longer because I have to go back and teach them the right way to do it and point out the obvious corners they cut." All those thoughts were the wrath of SM. SM judges others and measures her happiness on the spectrum of "enough." The true Emily does not.

When I gave myself the space to find the opposite truths that SM believed, I discovered remarkable things. For one, Achilles and I are the same. To make things better for both of us in the future I know what needs to be done. There are kinder and more efficient ways to motivate. I also saw that I don't have ungrateful children. They worked really hard and did not fight me on anything I asked them to do. Of course, children take longer than adults to clean or complete a task. They were doing their best. Achilles did care about me. He was following SM around the house with outstretched arms trying to hug her! I was the uncaring one.

SM helps me be the person I want to be because through her I can see the thoughts she has are not true. I know this because the thoughts she has are painful and stressful. When I choose to look back at the times I am not being the person I want to be and make a conscious plan to change my approach in the future, I find peace. Enough does not exist for me. What exists is a Scary Mommy and an Emily. Both are needed to receive a fullness of understanding and a fullness of joy.

Enough!

To me, constantly believing the lie that you aren't good enough or feeling bad about falling short equates to people who paid penance for their sins by whipping themselves with knotted cords and wrapping sharp chains around their legs. Some people may see or hear about this practice and say, "That's crazy! Why would anyone do that to themselves?" Then these same people walk around with the pains of thoughts of inadequacy whenever they fail and don't think that's crazy at all. Both are completely unnecessary. <u>What penance are you trying to pay by conforming to the idea that "I'm not good enough," and feeling bad about it? We misconstrue guilt as this cross we must carry to prove to God how sorry we are. The more guilty we feel the more humble we appear. That is not how atonement works.</u> The Atonement works to bring freedom through discovering truth. Guilt exists to get a person's attention that there is a need for change. Guilt is the wound and the atonement is the healing ointment. Guilt is for my good. It helps me know it's time to heal.

I know what it feels like thinking you aren't enough because I used to believe that. I would carry around that sadness everywhere. Now that I know it is never true...EVER...I won't entertain those thoughts again.

There is a louder voice now to advocate this idea that as women we are enough. It is a great message. However, being enough or not enough to me is a weak place to come from. Instead I want to be the person that says, "my best wasn't enough this time, but the good news is I can become better." There are always new skills to learn and ways to improve. Know that yes, you are enough, but sometimes my skill sets aren't. What an amazing distinction to know that there is no end to our potential!

Sane Mommy

The more I work the Atonement, the more I realize how Achilles and I are exactly the same. Achilles has always been a sensitive little guy. I remember him between 2-3 years old, drinking from a cup of milk (still getting the hang of it) and spilling the cup of milk. He reacted to the spill in a sort of panic, "Oh no, Oh no!" I would have to coach him through the spill by saying calmly, "It's no big deal," and urge him to say it with me. Through his whimpers he would sputter, "no big deal, no big deal." I was surprised at the reaction to spilled milk. Looking back, I can't remember ever raising my voice over something like a spill. I used to always laugh at the commercials when the kid would spill juice on the counter and the mom in the commercial would pause with a smile and slightly shake her head as to say, "oh, you." Then she would happily clean up the mess with the miracle paper towels she just bought - maybe cross her arms as she finished and do that side lean. It's nice to know that there are paper towels out there that have the ability to transform you into a perfectly patient parent. I doubt I was ever so happy to clean up a mess, but I know I never yelled if a spill happened, so I don't know where his panic would come from. It seemed he always just had this innate desire for perfection from the time he was little. As he grew and started school, he would often get frustrated at the need to erase a mistake. He would grunt and become agitated if things weren't turning out the way he hoped they would. I would ask him, "Why is it good to make mistakes on your homework?" He stumbled to find the answer I was looking for. With some help he eventually came to the conclusion that making mistakes on homework gave him the opportunity to practice so he could get better. I would emphasize this principle for him. I asked him, "When a baby is learning how to walk, does he get it perfect the first time or does he sometimes fall down?" He answered, "They fall down." "That's right, they fall down a lot!" I continued. "Practice is the only way people get better or learn anything new." Even now, if he gets overwhelmed, I see him stop, take his hand up to his chest with a big inhale, and push his hand down with an exhale, before continuing. Sometimes if he is especially upset, he will excuse himself to his room and sit on his bean bag chair for a few minutes to take a "time-out" which has become a term of chilling out in our house. I put myself in time-outs a lot. They are very helpful when you know you're headed in a downward spiral.

Achilles is so similar to me, in fact, that he's even developed negative beliefs similar to ones I have accumulated in the past. Whenever he has an inkling that he's "getting in trouble," he will either check-out of the conversation, or he will panic and cry. When he checks out, it's usually because I have started to lecture him about something. One time I was telling him that I was frustrated that he was leaving his clean laundry that I folded for him in the laundry basket instead of putting them away. The laundry basket became a dresser and the floor became his dirty laundry hamper. I was voicing my frustrations to him in the laundry room, and noticed his eyes slowly panning over to the map hanging on the wall. He muttered, "uh huh," at me and I lost my cool. SM emerged and clapped her hands as hard as she could 3 times while yelling, "YOU AREN'T LISTENING." Achilles, frightened by my clapping him back to attention, panicked and became defensive. With wide eyes he yelped, "Yes I was!" It was too late. SM had already escorted him out of the laundry room, using the door as a sort of broom. You know, like they use in ice curling? Not quite touching the stone, but getting pretty close. As the door closed on his face, he began to cry and retreated to his room. I was on the other side, holding my hands in my head, so disappointed in my reaction. It came 100% from believing in the thought that Achilles does not care about me, or about what I tell him. I believed he didn't care about what I do for him and that is why he left his clothes on the floor, and that is why he wasn't listening to me speak now.

I went to God and I questioned that lie, because it truly broke my heart knowing I hurt my sweet child's precious feelings. I wanted to make it right. God showed me the truth. I saw that Achilles does care about me, and that he does appreciate the things I do for him. When I was looking for evidence of this, a memory popped in my head of Achilles walking out to the kitchen to get a drink before hopping back into bed for the night. He saw me and said, "Wow, moms work really hard!" then drank his drink and returned to his room. He noticed! In that moment, without the story of him being lazy and ungrateful, I saw an 8-year-old boy, just doing what comes naturally. I also saw that I literally do what he does every day. I wash my clothes, put them in the hamper to be eventually folded, but put it off for days, just to have it transform into a dresser. I am exactly the same. Then I saw that I'm the one that really cares where the clothes go, so it's 100% my desire, not his. Now I know that Achilles does care about me and that it was me who wanted the clothes put away. The first thing I needed to do was apologize to him for being so cruel. After that, I could tell him that I am doing laundry for 5 people, and if he would be willing to put his laundry away when I ask, so that it's not more work for me, it would help me out so much. Achilles has always been willing to help me. I'm not coming from a place of "I'm right and you're wrong," but of a request from one human being to another to please help and contribute to the family.

That following Sunday I prayed to God to help me practice being more patient and uncovering the truth in the moment. The prayer was answered more quickly than I had anticipated. Achilles and Leah were playing hide and seek. Achilles had crawled under this small desk we were using as an office and pulled the desk chair as close to him as he could to keep himself hidden. When he pulled the chair in, he noticed the armrests would not fit as easily as he anticipated, so he attempted to lower the chair using the paddle on the side. Instead of lowering the chair, the chair raised up and took the desk drawers up with it. Realizing his error, he attempted to push the chair out from the drawers, not quite thinking through what would happen to a desk that is now tilted up and backwards. The chair shot out and the desk slammed onto the floor, which caused everything (the computer monitors, keyboards, microphones, etc.) to come crashing down.

Achilles immediately started screaming, "I'm sorry, I'm so sorry!!" Over and over. Loren rushed in to see if anyone was hurt, and to see if anything needed to be immediately moved to avoid further damage. I said nothing and walked the wailing Achilles back into his room to give him a chance to calm down. He continued to scream and cry over and over that he was so sorry. It was scary. I had never heard him so distraught. Other than a small scratch on the side panel of the modem, the computer and everything else that came down was fine. At this point, I didn't yet remember my prayer, but I did want to save Achilles from this very apparent suffering he was enduring. I grabbed my pen and legal pad and walked into his room as he was coming down from his upset. I didn't say a word. I just wrote. I was going to work the Atonement with Achilles the same way I worked it out with God (based on the Byron Katie, "Judge your neighbor" Worksheets).

The first thing I wrote down was the question, "What is your sad thought?"

A: I'm not helpful

E: What else?

A: I am frustrated because I got in trouble

So, I write down:

"I am in trouble," Is it true?

A: Yes

E: Can you absolutely know that it's true that you're in trouble?

A: No

E: How does the thought make you feel?

A: Sad, angry, frustrated

E: How do you react?

A: Scream, "I'm sorry," over and over

E: What is your body doing when you believe that you are in trouble?

A: Stressful, screaming and crying

E: Who would you be without the thought?

A: Happy, peaceful

E: What's the opposite of, "I'm in trouble."

A: I'm not in trouble

E: How is that true?

A: We all make mistakes. I say I'm sorry, and I really mean it.

I gave Achilles the opportunity to pinpoint the way it felt inside when you believe something that isn't true - that isn't from God. Then revealed the opposite feeling that must be from God, like peace.

Next, I continued to write down the conversation, but began to quietly respond as well.

A: But, I'm afraid something bad is going to happen.

E: Like what?

A: I'll have to pay with my own money.

E: How does that thought make you feel?

A: It makes me really sad and stressed out and angry.

E: What is your body doing?

A: My chest feels tight and I have trouble breathing. My throat hurts.

E: Who would you be without the thought?

A: My body wouldn't hurt

A: Happy that my apology was enough

I gave Achilles the opportunity to go deeper, past the original stressful thought. Things about what happened become clearer and were brought to his attention. As the lies (painful thoughts) were questioned, the truth came to light.

E: What's the opposite of "I have to pay"?

A: I don't have to pay

E: How is that true?

A: The screen was not broken when I saw it. Mom and Dad would not make me pay $2,000.

A: Maybe there's something I can do to fix it?

I recognized that Achilles began to see that without the fear of being in trouble (and running away), in his mind's eye he returned to the event and noticed other possibilities.

Loren came in the room at this point

E: So in that moment, what does "big trouble" mean?
A: I have to pay. I have to do something I don't like, like a punishment. Mom and Dad are angry and don't like me.

Achilles stopped and cried when he said that. I think he realized that this was the real BIG fear that was driving his reaction to the original thought that he was in big trouble.

E: Without that thought of being in big trouble, WHO WOULD YOU BE knowing things have fallen down?
A: Being Responsible - for what happened
E: What else?

A: Being Honest - telling dad what happened

E: What else?

A: Being Helpful - offering Dad help picking up the computer

E: Anything else?

A: That I'm really sorry for hurting Dad's computer, and I'll never play under the desk again."

E: Achilles, that was so sincere. Thank you. That was the first time I heard you say, "I'm sorry" and really mean it, because you weren't focused on yourself and being afraid of getting in trouble, but on the impact it had on Dad. That is so powerful.

Loren jumped in at this point to let Achilles know what was going on in his mind, that first and foremost he wanted to make sure that Achilles wasn't hurt, and second to see if anything needed immediate attention to prevent further damage. Because it didn't, Loren walked away from Achilles and the mess for a moment to calm down. He went on to say that there was NEVER a time when he stopped loving him. He was only worried because that's how he makes money for the family, and he was concerned the computer might be broken. He was never angry with him, just curious how it happened.

I then asked Achilles to explain what happened. He explained the step-by-step process, and I repeated back what I heard so I could get the right picture. It turned out that he saw Leah doing it moments before, and so he wanted to do the same. He just couldn't pull it off as delicately. Leah had already told Loren her part in the mess before Loren came into the bedroom. We then talked to both kids about it not being a good idea to play under the desk or in that area at all. They quickly agreed.

After everything settled down, I realized that this was the do-over I was praying for. I was given the opportunity to not believe a story about Achilles crashing a computer down, but instead, see my sweet child suffer and want to help him be free of the painful lies he was believing.

When he believed he had lost his parents' love I could see the pain on his face and feel it in my heart. I have felt the same thing, being worried about being in trouble because I ultimately feared that I would lose my parents' love and admiration. I needed their love to be happy. That was my focus, and I could tell that was also Achilles's focus in that moment. His loud display of suffering was not because he was sorry, it was a desperate plea for us to still love him. That's not to say he wasn't sorry, because I knew he was because he is such a sweet boy. He couldn't really be sorry, though, in that moment believing what he was believing.

When Achilles believed "If I show them my pain and how sorry I am, they won't be mad, and will still love me," it is just like me believing, "If I show Loren the pain he is causing me, he won't be mad and will still love me." Oh, how alike we are. Achilles gave me such amazing insight into my own heart by his willingness to share. I'm so grateful for that.

When I helped Achilles work through his thoughts, he saw that it wasn't until he knew he was believing a lie that he could really be himself, a person who is being responsible, honest, helpful, and sincerely apologetic and wanting to make things right. It was a powerful conversation. I wasn't talking AT Achilles I was talking WITH Achilles. I let him discover for himself the truth that he knew all along. True joy followed and we moved on with our life. He knew we loved him, because we love him unconditionally. Our love is not a light switch that turns off and on based on his actions. I love that he could see that truth for himself.

When our perspectives are focused on beliefs like, "I need your love." That's how we see the world. Love becomes contingent and the reactions of others become a personal attack on our identity. When our perspective is focused on the opposite "I want to give love," we are being our true selves; responsible, honest, helpful, apologetic, and humble. We cannot make right what we have wronged without having God's perspective of loving another. Otherwise, making right what we have wronged has an agenda of getting what we think we need. It is not real restitution and not real repentance. It's self-preservation - or preserving the lie that we have not yet questioned.

An Opportunity

Achilles and I are the same. We are both sensitive and seekers of perfection. We both fear the loss of love and long to be loved when we are believing the stressful thoughts that come to us. When I see him, I am seeing myself. I want to be kind because I want to be treated kindly. I want to be patient because I want others to be patient with me. I want to be talked with, not talked at and lectured.

I started saying a phrase to help Achilles (and myself) remember to question our thoughts when we've realized we have missed the mark. When I notice him starting to zone out, he's most likely believing the thought, "I don't want to get in trouble." I tell him: "Achilles, it's not about getting in trouble, it's about me giving you an opportunity to learn." It's inviting him to see it as a correcting or clarifying conversation with the perspective that mom's just doing her job. Her job is to teach and she does it because she cares about me and loves me.

Who Am I Being?

Focusing on this unmeasurable, mystical "enoughness" is not only a weak perspective, but it is a lie. What is enough? How can I be more than what I am being in the moment? So, if something happens that could cause me guilt, I instead think, "Darn it, I'm not being the mom I want to be." Then the conversation becomes, "God, I missed the mark here. I am not being patient and I am not being kind. I am not being unconditionally loving. <u>Help me see the lie I am believing that is preventing me from being who I know I truly am." I promise this one shift in thinking will transform the way you act in every way.</u> Seeking for perfection that results in feelings of inadequacy after failure causes suffering. It does not improve situations or make us better, because the focus is on the failure. Seeking for perfection that results in feelings of humility after failure causes peace. It comes from asking the question, "Who do I want to be?" We are filled with peace because we seek to counsel with God to help reveal our higher-selves that were temporarily hidden by stressful thoughts. I believe that's what it means to "be perfect in Christ." Perfection is found by seeking truth. Truth can only be found because it was once hidden.

Perfection

Viktor Frankl said, "Everyone has [his/her] own specific vocation or mission in life, everyone must carry out a concrete assignment that demands fulfillment. Therein [he/she] cannot be replaced nor can [his/her] life be repeated." My worth is not measured by what I can and can't do. I am valuable beyond measure for the simple fact that I WAS BORN! There is no one like me and there will never be anyone exactly like me again. Focus instead on living YOUR BEST LIFE and life will be worth living. The PERFECT life is possible, if you can see that it's possible.

I perfectly serve, every day as Christ asks us to serve. "For I am hungered, and ye gave me meat: I was thirsty, and ye gave me drink: I was a stranger, and ye took me in: Naked, and ye clothed me: I was sick, and ye visited me: I was in prison, and ye came unto me. Then shall the righteous answer him, saying, Lord, when saw we thee an hungered, and fed thee? or thirsty, and gave thee drink? When saw we thee a stranger, and took thee in? Or naked, and clothed thee? Or when saw we thee sick, or in prison, and came unto thee? And the King shall answer and say unto them, Verily I say unto you, Inasmuch as ye have done it unto one of the least of these my brethren, ye have done it unto me."[31]

---

[31] Matthew 25:35-40

My children came to me as strangers. The moment my children came out I held them, and then I fed them from my breasts, as they were hungry and thirsty. I continue to feed them and nourish their bodies. They came to me naked and I put that first onesie on them; perfectly new and clean - only the best. When my kids are sick, I care for them. I put the oils on their feet and do everything else in my power to ease their discomfort. When Achilles was in the hospital after his car accident, I sat by his bedside with him for 7 days. I cuddled with him and loved him up. When my children are in spiritual prison or they are believing stressful thoughts that are keeping them from being free, I go to them and teach them how to work the Atonement so that they too can be free. I teach them to look at the Devil's gift - the stressful thought - and ask for themselves if it is true or not.

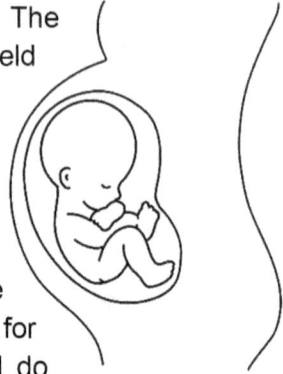

I know there are mothers who are purposely neglectful, but I'm not speaking to those mothers. Being perfect is easier than you may have thought. <u>You are perfection every day in your service and in seeking to be your best self.</u> Being perfect is not about never making mistakes or missing the mark. Being perfect in Christ is about knowing to use his Atonement, seeing with his eyes, and asking the question, "Am I being the person I want to be?" In all, perfection is about being a seeker of truth. It is not about having a lack of flaws. You are getting it right when you use the gift of the Devil and the Atonement together to change your heart. Perfection itself means complete. It's having the complete picture. That pain is needed for growth. That only through our missteps and mistakes are we able to see the truth. This is perfection.

CHAPTER 12

"Choose How You See"

What Is Shaping You?

Steven Covey said, "There is a mental creation, and a physical creation. The physical creation follows the mental, just as a building follows a blueprint. If you don't make a conscious effort to visualize who you are and what you want in life, then you empower other people and circumstances to shape you and your life by default." Creating who you want to be starts with your thoughts. It starts with what you believe is possible. If you allow the negative thoughts to shape you, every action taken is based on that perspective. You may not even be aware that your thoughts are shaping you because it's how it's always been.

When I was born, there were some complications. I was my mother's second child, first daughter, and first cesarean. The umbilical cord, my way of receiving nourishment, had become tangled and was wrapped around my neck and shoulder. With each contraction it became tighter and tighter. I was in trouble. Luckily, doctors were able to operate and rescue me in my time of need. Why did the umbilical cord wrap around my neck? I must have been somersaulting around and managed to get it all twisted up. I wasn't trying to hurt myself, I was just doing what babies do. When it comes to believing stressful thoughts, we are as innocent as babies in the womb. As growing humans, we twist and tangle our lines to God. Most of the time we are completely unaware that we are doing it. If we don't realize the lies we are believing that are causing us to sin, how are we to know we are in danger? When the grip of the cord becomes tight, like a noose around the neck, the baby's heart becomes stressed. It takes the hands of a skillful surgeon to go in, retrieve the child, and unravel the grip of that cord - the same cord meant to give nutrients. Does the baby tell herself, "I'm not good enough, I twisted up my cord." No. It only feels the distress of being choked and being cut off from oxygen.

Have you ever felt like you were being choked out by feelings of uneasiness? Have anxieties ever kept you up at night? Do you have regrets that follow you around? Are you angry or resentful toward anyone? If so, these thoughts are shaping who you are. You are a victim to life's circumstances. The good news is, you have to know what it feels like to be a victim in order to become unfettered from those thoughts that determine your state of being. That is the gift of the Devil.

The Gift of the Devil - Share the Stream

Your line to God has been tangled. The only way to untangle that line is by an outside source. To me that is Jesus Christ. He is my skillful surgeon. Together we look at the source of the tangle or knot to find out what message I am needing to be free.

Some may feel that the Devil is against us. I'd like to argue that the Devil is for us, whether He is aware of it or not. He is providing us a way to Christ. The only way to Christ. If we consider the Devil, the ego, or the natural man an enemy, our instinct may be to avoid the thoughts that are causing pain. I do not feel like this is how it is meant to be perceived.

Jesus taught, "Agree with thine adversary quickly, whiles thou art in the way with him lest at any time the adversary deliver thee to the judge, and the judge deliver thee to the officer, and thou be cast into prison."[32] Within the context of the scripture, one may read this as advice the Savior is giving to his disciples when it comes to the legal system. I feel it is also related to similar teachings that Jesus exemplified, principles such as loving your enemies, blessing them that curse you and doing good to them that hate you, etc. What does this mindset have to do with the Devil? Another word that describes the Devil is Adversary. An adversary is an opponent or rival. The Latin word for rival, rivalis, means "using the same stream as another."[33] When I think of this, I think of the phrase "a stream of thought," or, "stream of consciousness." These phrases describe the innumerable thoughts and feelings that move through the mind. In our own stream of thoughts is the Adversary, our rival, standing in that same stream. Using that stream for his own devices. In this stream, we are with him. Could Christ be urging us to agree with the opposition that is occupying our stream? The Latin word for agree is ad-gratus which means, "to please."[34] If I were to rewrite the scripture, respectfully it would read,

---

[32] Matthew 5:25
[33] "Rival: Definition of Lucifer by Oxford Dictionary on Lexico.com Also Meaning of Lucifer." *Lexico Dictionaries | English*, Lexico Dictionaries, 2020, www.lexico.com/en/definition/rival.
[34] "Agree: Definition of Lucifer by Oxford Dictionary on Lexico.com Also Meaning of Lucifer." *Lexico Dictionaries | English*, Lexico Dictionaries, 2020, www.lexico.com/en/definition/agree.

"Please the one that shares your stream of consciousness otherwise you will be cast into prison." Prison to me is the opposite of freedom. It is being tied down by anxieties and stressful beliefs. Therefore, freedom comes by pleasing the ever-present Devil. For me, pleasing the Devil means sharing the stream. It means dissecting the thought we catch to determine whether or not it is a true thought. If we avoid or fight those thoughts that cause discomfort, we will never be able to be free. The gift is being able to see the Devil in this light instead of something to fear. If Christ teaches us how to be "fishers of men," Satan teaches us how to be "fishers of thoughts." We can learn which thoughts need to be kept, and which thoughts should be thrown back. He is our fishing companion as we fish for thoughts in our stream of consciousness. Embrace the gift of negative and stressful thoughts; they are the key to your freedom. Those are the thoughts we take with us to Christ to be discussed, turned inside out, and analyzed. Great miracles will come of this process. They sure have for me.

Begin with The End in Mind

This life you have on earth is yours. You create it, from womb to tomb. Everything happens for you, not to you. Your relationships with others are for your good. The people you love the most have the ability to teach you the most.

What impact do you want to leave after you die? What is your legacy? Don't live a life on default, floating day by day, responding only to life's stimulus. Live with purpose. Choose your perspective. Create the kind of life you want for yourself. With God's help, He will open your eyes to your truest divine self, a higher-self already aligned to God's will.

Stephen Covey said, "Begin with the end in mind." We first need to know, or have faith, that in the end we will obtain peace of mind through the help of Christ. That's where Joy comes from. Believe that there is a force outside yourself that cares about you and wants you to have joy in your life. When your perspective is on believing that peace and joy are possible, that is exactly what will be.

See the world where an Adversary is a gift and not something to fear. See it as the way to a fullness of joy and understanding. See the world as a free person. Not as a victim. How will you choose to see the world?

Know Your Stumbling Blocks

Criticism makes me feel so small. Seeing Loren show anger or disappointment because I didn't live up to some kind of expectation in his mind is so aggravating and at the same time soul-crushing. Even if I work through the steps to turn around this stressful thought of criticism into: "he/she's being helpful or trying to make my life easier," there is still a ping of pain. I can't stand when people I love are disappointed with me. I'm a natural perfectionist. I have very high standards for myself. For reasons I don't understand, in childhood I really latched onto concepts that taught me to be a person to care first about another person's needs and feelings above my own. I learned quickly how never to offend anyone. I also strived diligently for praise. Getting A's in school and overachievement in academics was an obsession. I also had a high desire to be liked by all. Though this isn't a terrible thing, it did in many ways keep me from finding out who I was and the things I liked. It's hard to be authentic in your actions when you are more concerned and focused on how others will react.

Whenever I got yelled at as a child I would shut down. Thoughts would come to me like, "why do they only focus on the negative and not on ALL the good I do?" I believed that my failures should not be brought to my attention. It hurt me deeply. I didn't feel love in correction - except in the cases when I wanted to improve, like in my dancing. That kind of criticism was welcomed. I separated that from my persona. It wasn't an attack on my character or who I was as a person; it was feedback. It's the reason my dance team won awards. I liked school for the same reason. If I'd get a paper back covered with red ink and a poor grade, I could talk to my teacher and figure out where I went wrong so I could get a better grade next time. It was a growth mindset knowing that I could always improve, and it made me happy to see that improvement after hard work.

On the other hand, if I get criticized for the way I parent or the way that I keep house it really perturbs me. Being a mother is the most difficult job I've ever had. I feel like I should have the same mindset I did about dance and school - willing to receive feedback and a passion for growth. Unfortunately, it feels more like navigating through a minefield. I'm dealing with these little people who are different in every way. All of them! It's constant problem solving and creative thinking all custom crafted for one person - because I know the same thing won't necessarily work for another child. Motherhood is labor intensive and it's self-sacrificing. So, I believe that anything my husband or another person should offer me is nothing but positive praise. Have you ever been criticized by a stranger about the way you are parenting? I have, and it's incredibly annoying. When people share their opinion to me about how they think I could do a better job, I've learned to say, "Thank you" or "I'm sure you're right," then walk away. Of course, that's not the end of it. Thoughts run through my head defending myself and giving myself the benefit of the doubt. Though criticism from strangers can be annoying, anything sounding like it's coming from a place of frustration or anger from my husband, Loren, is debilitating for me. I get the same thoughts I did before as a child: "why do you only focus on the negative and not on ALL the good I do?"

If I take that statement and ask myself, "Emily, why does your thinking only focus on the negative and not all the good you do?" I remember something very important: because it's doing its job perfectly! My brain is following the process it was built on. I thought that one day I would be able to completely reprogram it so that nothing would bother me. Criticisms from those I love would just roll down my back, and I would be immune and have everlasting peace. It was frustrating because I had been using the gift of the Devil and Atonement of Christ and had been discovering remarkable truths, but in many cases, this was the one thing that kept coming back. I felt I could never escape from it.

Then it hit me. This stumbling block is the one thing I must pay attention to the most. This stumbling block of mine is really my podium. I just found my PURPOSE through the biggest struggle I have. Makes sense - if the gift of the Devil is meant to show me truth through the opposite, <u>it will magnify my greatest potential and impact by making it into the most feared or most painful thing to me!</u>

We love Stephen Covey if you haven't guessed already. We even named our 4th child after him. In his book, Covey said, "Be a light, not a judge. Be a model, not a critic. Be part of the solution, not part of the problem."[35] I was afraid to write a book

---

[35] Covey, Stephen R. *The 7 Habits of Highly Effective People.* FranklinCovey Co., 2016.

that was this transparent. I am opening myself up to lots of criticism. Because I know that this is my greatest fear, I also know it is incredibly important that I do it. In all, if I want to be part of the solution (be a light), I must contribute to the solution - even if it pains me to do it.

Suffer

Mother Teresa ministered to hundreds, if not thousands, of poor and dying people in the streets of Calcutta. She wrote many letters to her spiritual confidant, the Rev. Michael van der Peet about her crisis of faith. In these letters she expressed the intense loneliness that she felt while in her ministry work. She felt like God was not with her in the work and at many times was stuck in feelings of depression and sorrow. She talked about feeling like she was in the depths of Hell and that the smile she put on her face was sometimes just for show, for she was truly struggling with this darkness inside her. At times she felt that Christ was absent from her life, "[But] as for me, the silence and the emptiness is so great, that I look and do not see,--Listen and do not hear--the tongue moves [in prayer] but does not speak ... I want you to pray for me--that I let Him have [a] free hand."[36] Why would someone who clearly felt the call to serve and felt a passion for sitting with the poor and dying feel this intense loneliness? You would think she would only feel validation and support for such a cause. I can never know for sure, but Mother Teresa surrounded herself with the loneliest of people. She saw them and knew the importance of serving "the least of these." She knew her purpose. It spoke to her heart that said that no one should die alone. For many of these poor people, that's exactly what

[36] Biema, David Van. "Mother Teresa's Crisis of Faith." *Time*, 2007, time.com/4126238/mother-teresas-crisis-of-faith/.

happened. In India where there is still an unspoken caste system (even though outlawed today), people are labeled "untouchable" because they are poor or sick, and are often left to die alone. Would she have been able to fulfil her greatest calling if she could not understand what these people were feeling? Not only did she make sure these people were not physically alone as she held their hand to die, but they were also not emotionally alone. She could feel what they were feeling. These intense feelings of loneliness were a gift to her to be able to connect. She had to feel this separation from God to know what it truly felt like to be alone. Her life dedicated to service was a passionate one. Passion literally means to suffer. Compassion means to suffer with. If doing what we love requires suffering, pain, and anguish, then you know you are on the right path.

Mother Teresa was also not immediately welcomed into the streets of Calcutta. You'd think, how can anyone be against what she was doing? It was such pure and wonderful work! However, there were people who did not want her there. They did not want her religion there or her help. She was often met with protest or opposition. That is why it is so important to know who you are and be certain about your purpose and your personal mission on the earth. Otherwise, you suffer - not through joy, but through painful thoughts of how others see you.

Create Who You Want to Be

A guru named Sadhguru said, "Only when you do not know yourself, the opinion of others become important." When we know who we are and know what our purpose is, it won't matter what others think. It's much too important! It becomes the beacon to focus on. If someone, especially in a public space, is accusatory or says something towards me that bothers me, I can check my values and make sure that I am honoring who I am. If I am, then their comment can be tossed out. It may still hurt to hear, but when you turn your attention inward and ask yourself, "Did I speak from the heart? Did my comment reflect my values and personal mission?" the answers will help you know next steps. If the answers are yes, then move on. If, no, then make it right with yourself.

No one can ever see the real you anyway. People see what they have created in their minds based on their own beliefs and values. One person may think they love me while another thinks they hate me. <u>We are not dealing with people. We are dealing with thoughts.</u> Our thoughts may sound a lot like us, but they are not us. Because of the way our brains operate, thoughts serve one purpose - to judge. Believing those judgements, whether they be kind or critical is our choice.

No matter where you came from, who your parents were or are, or what you think your identity is, it can all change. Lisa Bilyeu, the co-founder and president of Impact Theory, a media company focused on growth mindset and empowerment content as well as the co-founder of the billion-dollar brand, Quest Nutrition, will often speak about this topic. She says, "evolve so hard they have to get to know you again." Evolve so much that you need to reintroduce yourself to people that have known you for years! We must know who we are in order to know what we want from this life. I want to be no one - I want to only be walking values. Have you created and declared who you are? Have you ever sat down and wrote the values that are most important to you? Do you know who you are?

CHAPTER 13

"Creating A Personal Declaration"

The purpose of creating a personal declaration is for you. It's to know who you are and what you want to create for yourself in your life. It is meant to be reviewed often so that it is at the forefront of your mind. Memorize it; write it on your heart.

First, start with values that speak to you. There are lists of thousands of values you can sift through online. Pick the ones that you want to emulate always and that you want to be known for. Next, write down who you want to be as an individual and then how you want to be for others. This includes your closest relationships. When you write this declaration, write it as if it has already happened. This is who you really are. When you are not living true to who you know you are you will feel it and be able to course correct. Keep it close to you always. Update it and change it as you change and grow yourself. In the spirit of one of my values, vulnerability, I will share my personal declaration with you.

I am Emily Ayars Schilt Smith. I am an elect lady; daughter of a Heavenly Father. I am the creator of my world with Christ as my compass. I am a disciple of Jesus Christ. I am gratitude. I see beauty in the world and cherish it. I am strong shoulders to stand on. I am empathy and love. I meet others where they are on their journey and honor God within them. Everyone feels safe, seen, and appreciated when they are with me. I am a fullness of joy. Infinite knowledge is available to me and I continuously seek to learn and evolve. I am vulnerable and speak from the heart. I am generous and share all I have. I am a fierce friend. Divine love is felt in my touch and in my smile. My words have the power to heal hearts. I am head over heels in love with my sexy, intelligent, hungry-for-life husband, Loren Paul Smith. I am patient, kind, loving and respectful, especially to Loren Smith and to my children. I am here for others and serve incredibly. I am perfect health. My body is breathtaking, beautiful and a miracle. I am light. I am whole.

This is me. This is me without my thoughts. When I am not being who I know I am, I will not feel at peace. But how wonderful! <u>The lack of peace will show me the way back!</u>

There is one more declaration I wish to share. It is our family declaration. It hangs in our house to remind us who we are and what our purpose is as a family.

Smith Family Declaration

The purpose of our family is to SERVE and INSPIRE. As members of the Smith Family, we are committed to living values that emulate this purpose.

BEING

We, as a family, are **loyal** to one another and to God. We support each other and serve each other, as well as align our will with God's. We are **humble** in all things. We concurrently stand for being honest and vulnerable (this includes being honest with ourselves). This takes courage, a trait in which we all possess. When we share we speak from the heart. We know that by telling all our heart we will be able to **inspire** and touch the hearts of others. We are always being our best, boldly going forward with confidence in who we are - that we are perfect in Christ - and that there is no mistake in this.

SEEING

We are creators of possibility. We create the world in which we live; we create the lives we want for ourselves; we see that there are unlimited resources available to us to achieve the possibilities that we create; and we act in faith to achieve all things. Through our eyes we see that life is a gift, and each breath is taken with **gratitude** and thankfulness. We live **Sapere Vedere**; we know how to see. We see the truth, that God is good. We practice **Namaste**; we see and honor God within everyone. When we listen to others we do so **empathetically**. We walk with them through their journey, and meet them where they are. We know that in them we really see ourselves.

DOING

There is no ideal we need to strive for or hope to become. We know that all we can be is who we are in the present moment. Whilst in the present moment, we do things that inspire continuous improvement (**Kaizen**) and we seek for truth in every thought. We have the freedom to explore and inquire in all things. We live **adventurously** and spontaneously, experiencing all this beautiful world has to offer us. We **serve** all, giving generously (things that never belonged to us in the first place). We are **passionate** about, and do great work in, our service and in our contribution to the world.

Our home is where EVERYONE belongs. No one is greater than another. We practice **Genshai**; never acting in a way that would make someone feel small. We love unconditionally, and are kind to others as well as ourselves. We forgive when we have been hurt and forgive ourselves when we have hurt ourselves or others - making amends and always thanking the experience for showing us how to live! By this we live and leave a **legacy** of leadership, making a difference in the world through peace and love. In all, Christ is the center of our family. We are here to SERVE and INSPIRE others as He did in his earthly ministry - together.

Create Values

As a family, we highlight one value a month with service always in accompaniment. These values are often the topic of conversation as we make connections to them and find our way back to them if we have strayed. Clear family and personal values create clear paths towards the end goal: Heaven on Earth. Peace is possible now, even if you've endured the hardest of hardships.

Two Words

The Devil's role is indispensable. It is meant to be a powerful tool. Use it and gain your freedom. This life is a gift. There are those who may be destined to have more suffering in this life than others. I was born in a country where I have access to education, healthcare, and unlimited resources to succeed. If I have stumbling blocks, they are from my own creation. Knowing this, it is incredibly clear to me that I am meant to ease suffering, offer my support, and extend a loving hand to all I meet. I know my purpose. It is written on my heart. I have narrowed it down to two words - words I will keep close and ponder. Do you know your purpose? Do you know who you are? Write it down. Print it out. Put it into practice.

Peace in the Opposite

The Devil's role is indispensable. He is the only reason a Savior exists. He marks the path that leads the way to Christ - to freedom. It is the only way. You can create the life you want instead of the life you have been conditioned to live. You can find peace if you turn to the opposite - to those persistent painful thoughts that keep you down - and question them. In them lies the power to be free, and in control, once and for all. I respect and love the role of the Devil. It is truly a gift.

www.ingramcontent.com/pod-product-compliance
Lightning Source LLC
LaVergne TN
LVHW052026080426
835513LV00018B/2187